Abortion

Other Books of Related Interest

Opposing Viewpoints Series

Gendercide

Sexual Violence

Teen Dating

At Issue Series

Age of Consent

Are Abortion Rights Threatened?

Embryonic and Adult Stem Cells

Current Controversies Series

Medical Ethics

"Congress shall make no law . . . abridging the freedom of speech, or of the press."

First Amendment to the US Constitution

The basic foundation of our democracy is the First Amendment guarantee of freedom of expression. The Opposing Viewpoints Series is dedicated to the concept of this basic freedom and the idea that it is more important to practice it than to enshrine it.

Elizabeth Des Chenes, *Director, Content Strategy*
Douglas Dentino, *Manager, New Product*

For more information, contact:
Greenhaven Press
27500 Drake Rd.
Farmington Hills, MI 48331-3535
Or you can visit our Internet site at gale.cengage.com

For product information and technology assistance, contact us at

Gale Customer Support, 1-800-877-4253
For permission to use material from this text or product, submit all requests online at www.cengage.com/permissions

Further permissions questions can be emailed to permissionrequest@cengage.com

Articles in Greenhaven Press anthologies are often edited for length to meet page requirements. In addition, original titles of these works are changed to clearly present the main thesis and to explicitly indicate the author's opinion. Every effort is made to ensure that Greenhaven Press accurately reflects the original intent of the authors. Every effort has been made to trace the owners of copyrighted material.

Cover image copyright © Smit/Shutterstock.com.

LIBRARY OF CONGRESS CATALOGING-IN-PUBLICATION DATA

Abortion / Noël Merino, book editor.
        p. cm. -- (Opposing viewpoints)
    Includes bibliographical references and index.
    ISBN 978-0-7377-6939-5 (hardcover) -- ISBN 978-0-7377-6940-1 (pbk.)
    1. Abortion. 2. Abortion--Moral and ethical aspects. 3. Abortion--Law and legislation. I. Merino, Noël, editor of compilation.
    HQ767.A1535 2013
    362.1988'8--dc23
                                                                        2013037282

Printed in the United States of America
1 2 3 4 5 6 7 18 17 16 15 14

Contents

Chapter 3: Should Abortion Rights Be Restricted?

Chapter 4: What Are Some Medical and Social Concerns About Abortion?

Why Consider Opposing Viewpoints?

> *"The only way in which a human being can make some approach to knowing the whole of a subject is by hearing what can be said about it by persons of every variety of opinion and studying all modes in which it can be looked at by every character of mind. No wise man ever acquired his wisdom in any mode but this."*
>
> John Stuart Mill

In our media-intensive culture it is not difficult to find differing opinions. Thousands of newspapers and magazines and dozens of radio and television talk shows resound with differing points of view. The difficulty lies in deciding which opinion to agree with and which "experts" seem the most credible. The more inundated we become with differing opinions and claims, the more essential it is to hone critical reading and thinking skills to evaluate these ideas. Opposing Viewpoints books address this problem directly by presenting stimulating debates that can be used to enhance and teach these skills. The varied opinions contained in each book examine many different aspects of a single issue. While examining these conveniently edited opposing views, readers can develop critical thinking skills such as the ability to compare and contrast authors' credibility, facts, argumentation styles, use of persuasive techniques, and other stylistic tools. In short, the Opposing Viewpoints Series is an ideal way to attain the higher-level thinking and reading skills so essential in a culture of diverse and contradictory opinions.

In addition to providing a tool for critical thinking, Opposing Viewpoints books challenge readers to question their own strongly held opinions and assumptions. Most people form their opinions on the basis of upbringing, peer pressure, and personal, cultural, or professional bias. By reading carefully balanced opposing views, readers must directly confront new ideas as well as the opinions of those with whom they disagree. This is not to argue simplistically that everyone who reads opposing views will—or should—change his or her opinion. Instead, the series enhances readers' understanding of their own views by encouraging confrontation with opposing ideas. Careful examination of others' views can lead to the readers' understanding of the logical inconsistencies in their own opinions, perspective on why they hold an opinion, and the consideration of the possibility that their opinion requires further evaluation.

Evaluating Other Opinions

To ensure that this type of examination occurs, Opposing Viewpoints books present all types of opinions. Prominent spokespeople on different sides of each issue as well as well-known professionals from many disciplines challenge the reader. An additional goal of the series is to provide a forum for other, less known, or even unpopular viewpoints. The opinion of an ordinary person who has had to make the decision to cut off life support from a terminally ill relative, for example, may be just as valuable and provide just as much insight as a medical ethicist's professional opinion. The editors have two additional purposes in including these less known views. One, the editors encourage readers to respect others' opinions—even when not enhanced by professional credibility. It is only by reading or listening to and objectively evaluating others' ideas that one can determine whether they are worthy of consideration. Two, the inclusion of such viewpoints encourages the important critical thinking skill of objectively evaluating an author's credentials and bias. This evaluation will illuminate an author's reasons for taking a particular stance on an issue and will aid in readers' evaluation of the author's ideas.

It is our hope that these books will give readers a deeper understanding of the issues debated and an appreciation of the complexity of even seemingly simple issues when good and honest people disagree. This awareness is particularly important in a democratic society such as ours in which people enter into public debate to determine the common good. Those with whom one disagrees should not be regarded as enemies but rather as people whose views deserve careful examination and may shed light on one's own.

Thomas Jefferson once said that "difference of opinion leads to inquiry, and inquiry to truth." Jefferson, a broadly educated man, argued that "if a nation expects to be ignorant and free . . . it expects what never was and never will be." As individuals and as a nation, it is imperative that we consider the opinions of others and examine them with skill and discernment. The Opposing Viewpoints Series is intended to help readers achieve this goal.

David L. Bender and Bruno Leone,
Founders

Introduction

"You've heard this is all going to mean government funding of abortion. Not true."

—Barack Obama,
President of the United States,
August 19, 2009

Abortion has been a polarizing issue in the United States since the US Supreme Court ruled that women have the right to abortion in 1973. For the last couple of decades, Gallup polls have found the country almost evenly divided between those who consider themselves "pro-choice" and those who consider themselves "pro-life." Not surprisingly, then, public support for government funding of abortion is also hotly debated.

After *Roe v. Wade* was decided, US Representative Henry Hyde sponsored a bill prohibiting the use of federal funds to pay for abortions. Since 1976, the Hyde Amendment has been attached to the annual federal spending bill every year, prohibiting the use of federal funds within the bill from being used for abortions, with limited exceptions. The exceptions change from year to year depending on the political views of the members of Congress, but always include the exception of when the pregnant woman's life is at stake and sometimes include other exceptions, such as when pregnancy results from rape or incest.

Since abortion is a medical procedure, many women cover the cost of abortion through their health insurance. For women who have health insurance or medical care through the federal government, however, the Hyde Amendment's restriction on federal funding precludes the use of their federal health care benefits for abortion. This means that low-income women covered by Medicaid, women covered by federal health insurance due to government employment, women in federal prison, and women receiving health care from Indian Health Services cannot use insurance to cover the cost of abortion. In about a third of the states, state funds are used to cover abortion for women who are insured by Medicaid.

With the passage of the Patient Protection and Affordable Care Act (PPACA), signed into law in 2010, the debate about government funding of abortion was reignited. Under PPACA, insurance exchanges are set up in states where only approved plans can be sold and where government subsidies are provided to make insurance more affordable for those who need it. The government involvement with the exchanges raised concern about possible government funding of abortion.

In order to avoid government funding of abortion, Section 1303 of PPACA requires a segregation of funds used for abortion. States are required under PPACA to offer at least one health plan that does not offer abortion services. For states with insurance plans that cover abortion and for people who elect this coverage, the law requires that a separate fee of at least a dollar be paid to a separate account, in order to assure that no federal or state dollars are use to fund abortion services. The Barack Obama administration enacted this requirement to avoid government funding of abortions, but not everyone agrees that it achieves this end.

The US Conference of Catholic Bishops responded to Section 1303 with the following statement: "Some will say this is technically not 'tax funding of abortions,' because the required surcharge will be a premium payment rather than a tax payment as such. But what the payment is called is less important than what it actually does." On the other side of the debate, there is concern that the way PPACA addresses abortion is bad policy for women. NARAL Pro-Choice America says of the plan:

Offering women the "option" to pay extra for supplemental abortion coverage, often known as a rider policy, is a false promise. Unintended pregnancies are by definition unplanned; women rarely purchase abortion coverage in anticipation of these circumstances. In fact, there is little evidence that insurers even offer these products. Women should not be denied coverage for basic reproductive-health services by politicians imposing their personal agendas on private medical decisions.

With opposition on both sides of the abortion debate, Section 1303 of PPACA seems to have failed as an adequate compromise.

The public is divided over the issue of abortion. The debates about government funding of abortion and other issues are likely to continue for some time. Opposing viewpoints on a variety of abortion-related issues are offered in *Opposing Viewpoints: Abortion* under the following chapter titles: Is Abortion Immoral?, What Has Been the Impact of *Roe v. Wade?*, Should Abortion Rights Be Restricted?, and What Are Some Medical and Social Concerns About Abortion? The views in this anthology offer different perspectives on these issues and illustrate the high level of social divergence on this controversial issue.

OPPOSING
VIEWPOINTS®
SERIES

I Is Abortion Immoral?

Chapter Preface

The debate about the morality of abortion centers on two distinct questions: (1) When does personhood begin? and (2) What moral duties, if any, does a pregnant woman have toward her fetus? The answers to both of these questions will not solve the question of the morality of abortion without other premises, but the controversy regarding the morality of abortion usually results from disagreement about the answers to these two questions.

The question of when personhood begins can be understood as either a physical or metaphysical question. If personhood is simply a matter of physical facts, then presumably science can answer the question of when personhood begins. Different biological stages may be suggested as possible markers of personhood, including the point at which a human egg is fertilized, the point at which a fertilized egg implants itself in the lining of a woman's uterus, the stage in pregnancy when the fetus develops a heartbeat, at the first appearance of fetal brain waves, the stage at which the fetus feels pain, the moment of birth, or even at some developmental stage of the baby after birth. Although at most of these stages people might agree that life is present, the question of whether a person exists is hotly debated. Life alone is not necessarily a morally relevant category: for example, plants are alive, but not many people would argue that this creates a moral reason against destroying or eating them. Thus, the question about personhood appears to be one that cannot be easily reduced to physical facts that science can resolve.

If the question of personhood is a metaphysical one, then the answers are to be found in religion or philosophy. Competing answers have been put forth by different religions and philosophical belief systems for centuries with little agreement except perhaps that most (but not all) take the moment of birth to be the latest point at which the fetus becomes a person. A large part of the debate about abortion today is where to draw this line about personhood, and little consensus exists.

Even if agreement could be reached on the issue of personhood, abortion deals with a situation not readily mimicked elsewhere, since the fetus is inside the pregnant woman. Thus, even among people who believe that personhood starts at conception, not all conclude that this means abortion is immoral. This is because even if it is agreed that innocent persons should not be killed, women have rights that may not make the killing of a fetus morally wrong. In the extreme case where pregnancy will result in the death of the pregnant woman, the issue literally pits one life against the other. In this case, actually, there is a certain degree of consensus that abortion is morally permissible. However, where the woman's life is not at stake, there is widespread disagreement about whether or not she has a moral duty to refrain from killing the fetus within her, or whether her rights outweigh any considerations about the life of the fetus.

The debate about the morality of abortion is one that involves resolving two very complicated issues: the question of when morally relevant life, or personhood, begins; and the question of what rights a woman has vis-à-vis a fetus growing inside her. In the following chapter the authors debate both of these questions, which lead them to different conclusions about the morality of abortion.

❚ *"Roe represents tragedy."*

Roe v. Wade: Four Decades of Tragedy

Doug Bandow

In the following viewpoint Doug Bandow argues that the legalization of abortion in Roe v. Wade *in 1973 created a tragedy by allowing women's liberty to triumph over human life. Bandow contends that a serious justification is needed to end a human life and argues that those who defend abortion for any reason are stuck defending abortion for sex selection, which he claims is of a form of violence against women. He concludes that the issue of sex selection has helped to turn more Americans against abortion without restrictions. Bandow is a senior fellow at the Cato Institute who specializes in foreign policy and civil liberties.*

As you read, consider the following questions:

1. According to Bandow, abortion is not a choice but a what?

2. What seven countries does the author cite as having obvious preferences for male children?

3. According to Bandow, what do the majority of Americans think about sex-selection abortion?

Roe v. Wade, perhaps the most ostentatiously unconstitutional of many dubious Supreme Court decisions purporting to interpret the Constitution, was issued 40 years ago. Rather than settle the abortion issue, the justices triggered a bitter political conflict which continues unabated.

Roe represents tragedy. An unwanted pregnancy can cause serious, sometimes overwhelming, problems. Moreover, there are few more personal decisions than to terminate a pregnancy. Liberty and life seemingly come into sharp conflict.

But abortion is not a just another "choice." Rather, it is a flight from responsibility. Abortion is a response to choice, that is, the decision to have sex. Other than rape, sex is voluntary. Sometimes the result is an unwanted baby.

The question then is what to do? What is a person's responsibility for the earlier choice freely exercised? Abortion has become a leading means to avoid taking responsibility for the life created.

This goes as much for men as well as women. In fact, many of the most fervent abortion supporters are men. The availability of abortion absolves them of responsibility for their actions. Lynn Marie Kohm of Regent University School of Law observed: "Indeed, the ultimate irony of abortion is that it inherently lets men off the hook."

Pregnancy produces a human being. Arcane arguments over personhood do not change the fact that the continuum of life is not easily segmented. Whether the critical moment is conception or implantation, thus starts a process which, if not interrupted, results in a human being. The physical differences between a fetus, a baby, and a child, though real, do not affect the moral worth of the individual created. No one should be aborted without serious, if not overwhelming, justification.

There is one when the mother's life is at stake. But not because someone would prefer not to have a baby at a particular

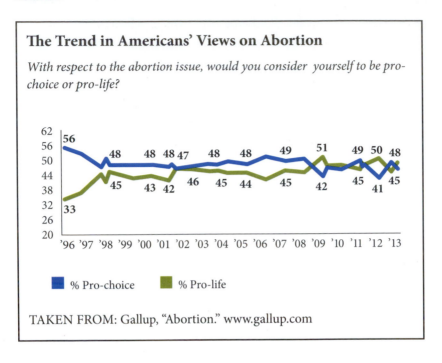

The Trend in Americans' Views on Abortion

With respect to the abortion issue, would you consider yourself to be pro-choice or pro-life?

■ % Pro-choice   ■ % Pro-life

TAKEN FROM: Gallup, "Abortion." www.gallup.com

time. The claim that abortion is an absolute right even when the pregnancy results from voluntary sex sacrifices life for convenience. For instance, last year [2012] blogger Allison Benedikt waxed eloquent in defending the right to kill one's baby because one is a newlywed and not yet "ready for kids," a "single woman who wants to focus on her career," or "the mother of two who is not in the market for number three." All of these would be good reasons to eschew sex. Certainly they justify using birth control. And they create an understandable desire not to be pregnant. But they are not good reasons to eliminate a life, especially with adoption as an alternative.

Yet there is at least one worse reason to abort a baby: sex selection. You want a kid. But you want a kid of a particular sex, usually male. Unfortunately, even with modern technology it's hard to guarantee the result. No problem, argued Benedikt, who warned her pro-abortion allies against feeling guilty. Just kill the (mostly) female babies. After all, "these are fetuses with female or male genitals—not little girls and little boys."

Some people don't even make that distinction. Princeton "ethicist" Peter Singer is not the only educated professional to advocate infanticide. Last year Alberto Giubilini and Francesca Minerva argued in the *Journal of Medical Ethics* for what they called "after-birth abortion" if the circumstances "would have justified abortion." Presumably having to purchase pink rather than blue baby clothing could create just such a burden. So solve that problem with a sex-based abortion. After all, "Merely being human is not in itself a reason for ascribing someone a right to life," wrote Giubilini and Minerva.

Nevertheless, even most abortion advocates don't go this far. For them, birth means something. And being a human being *does* create a right to life. Frances Kissling, a long-time abortion advocate with Catholics for Choice, admitted: "Abortion is not like having your tooth pulled or having your appendix out. It involves the termination of an early form of human life. That deserves some gravitas."

But abortion supporters still are stuck with sex selection abortion. No matter that sex discrimination is widely thought to be bad. If abortion is an absolute right, then the reason doesn't matter, even if the purpose is to kill baby girls.

The problem isn't theoretical. The child-gender ratio in India, which recently has been convulsed in outrage over a murderous gang rape, "is at its most lopsided in 50 years," reported the *Washington Post* earlier this month [January 2013]. Some of the lowest ratios of females to males occur in cities and provinces populated by the growing middle class. Observed the *Post*: "a growing number of couples opt to abort female fetuses or neglect infant girls in their desperation for sons."

China may pose an even greater problem. The age-old preference for boys—who provide farm labor and carry the family name—has been aggravated by the Maoist regime's "one-child" policy. Although that restriction has been relaxed, China now has a dramatically malformed age and sex structure. Normal is 105 boys to 100 girls; in some provinces the ratio climbs above 130. A deadly preference for males also is found in Afghanistan, Bangladesh, Pakistan, South Korea, and Taiwan. All told, Mara Hvistendahl, author of *Unnatural Selection: Choosing Boys Over Girls, and the Consequences of a World Full of Men*, estimates that Asia lacks 160 million women who otherwise would be alive.

A similar phenomenon is evident in Armenia, Azerbaijan, Kosovo, and elsewhere in Eastern Europe. Some immigrant-heavy Canadian provinces exhibit a similar pattern, as do America's ethnic Chinese, Indian, and Korean populations. Indeed, Kohm argued that "Sex selection abortion, or sex preselection as it may also be labeled, is rapidly becoming an acceptable family planning alternative for Americans."

Kohm went on to call the practice "woman-on-woman violence." If it is a woman's choice to have an abortion, then sex selection abortion usually means women (adults) killing women (babies). That is, complained Kohm, women "insist on putting self desire for a child of a certain sex above common good to all women by aborting female fetuses."

But sex selection and the culture behind the practice give rise to violence against adult females as well. In developing states mothers known to be carrying girls sometimes face physical abuse, often in an attempt to induce an abortion. The lack of brides for "excess" males has created a veritable industry in sex trafficking throughout East Asia, especially to China and Taiwan, some of it forced. Harvard's Erika Christakis pointed to the Indian rape as another, even more brutal, possible consequence: "the preference for male babies in India and much of the world may be at the root of this senseless violence." Although correlation does not prove causation, the "rates of violence towards women increase" in nations as their male to female gender ratios increase, she explained.

There are other adverse social consequences. Warned Christakis: "The imbalance has squeezed poor and uneducated men out of the marriage market in particular, so there is a surplus of young men who are unable to find partners and assume standard adult roles in their societies." Their frustration could even turn into fodder for social unrest and foreign conflict.

Forty years ago pro-abortion advocates won the battle of *Roe v. Wade*. But they short-circuited the political process, effectively jump-starting the vibrant pro-life movement. In recent years more people have declared themselves to be pro-life than pro-choice, and the majority of Americans oppose unrestricted abortion. The vast majority dislike sex selection abortion. The pro-abortion lobby may ultimately lose the political war.

No where is the tension between liberty and life more obvious than the issue of abortion. Yet the real issue is responsibility, not choice. One must take responsibility for one's actions to preserve liberty. Which in the case of abortion means protecting, not destroying, life.

> "*[A woman's] life and what is right for her circumstances and her health should automatically trump the rights of the non-autonomous entity inside of her. Always.*"

The Choice to Abort Is Up to Women

Mary Elizabeth Williams

In the following viewpoint Mary Elizabeth Williams argues that even if a fetus is a human life, that does not mean that abortion is morally wrong. Williams contends that too many pro-choice advocates deny the human life of the fetus or end up drawing irrelevant lines in fetal development between nonlife and life. But Williams claims that a fetus does constitute human life and yet argues that the life of the mother always trumps the life of the fetus such that she may choose abortion. Williams is a staff writer for Salon, *an online magazine.*

As you read, consider the following questions:

1. The author claims that opponents of abortion have co-opted what word?

Mary Elizabeth Williams, "So What If Abortion Ends Life?" *Salon*, January 23, 2013. This article first appeared on Salon.com, at http://www.Salon.com. An online version remains in the Salon archives. Reprinted with permission.

2. According to Williams, in what situations do the rights of a woman outweigh the rights of her fetus?

3. What four examples does Williams give of situations where people in the United States make choices about life?

Of all the diabolically clever moves the anti-choice lobby has ever pulled, surely one of the greatest has been its consistent co-opting of the word "life." Life! Who wants to argue with that? Who wants be on the side of—not-life? That's why the language of those who support abortion has for so long been carefully couched in other terms. While opponents of abortion eagerly describe themselves as "pro-life," the rest of us have had to scramble around with not nearly as big-ticket words like "choice" and "reproductive freedom." The "life" conversation is often too thorny to even broach. Yet I know that throughout my own pregnancies, I never wavered for a moment in the belief that I was carrying a human life inside of me. I believe that's what a fetus is: a human life. And that doesn't make me one iota less solidly pro-choice.

All Life Is Not Equal

As *Roe v. Wade* [1973] enters its fifth decade, we find ourselves at one of the most schizo moments in our national relationship with reproductive choice. In the past year [2012] we've endured the highest number of abortion restrictions ever. Yet support for abortion rights is at an all-time high, with seven in 10 Americans in favor of letting *Roe v. Wade* stand, allowing for reproductive choice in all or "most" cases. That's a stunning 10 percent increase from just a decade ago. And in the midst of this unique moment, Planned Parenthood has taken the bold step of reframing the vernacular—moving away from the easy and easily divisive words "life" and "choice." Instead, as a new promotional film acknowledges, "It's not a black and white issue."

It's a move whose time is long overdue. It's important, because when we don't look at the complexities of reproduction, we give far too much semantic power to those who'd try to control it. And we play into the sneaky, dirty tricks of the anti-choice lobby when we on the pro-choice side squirm so uncomfortably at the ways in which they've repeatedly appropriated the concept of "life."

Here's the complicated reality in which we live: All life is not equal. That's a difficult thing for liberals like me to talk about, lest we wind up looking like death-panel-loving, kill-your-grandma-and-your-precious-baby storm troopers. Yet a fetus can be a human life without having the same rights as the woman in whose body it resides. She's the boss. Her life and what is right for her circumstances and her health should automatically trump the rights of the non-autonomous entity inside of her. Always.

When we on the pro-choice side get cagey around the life question, it makes us illogically contradictory. I have friends who have referred to their abortions in terms of "scraping out a bunch of cells" and then a few years later were exultant over the pregnancies that they unhesitatingly described in terms of "the baby" and "this kid." I know women who have been relieved at their abortions and grieved over their miscarriages. Why can't we agree that how they felt about their pregnancies was vastly different, but that it's pretty silly to pretend that what was growing inside of them wasn't the same? Fetuses aren't selective like that. They don't qualify as human life only if they're intended to be born.

The Relevance of Life

When we try to act like a pregnancy doesn't involve human life, we wind up drawing stupid semantic lines in the sand: first trimester abortion vs. second trimester vs. late term, dancing around the issue trying to decide if there's a single magic moment when a fetus becomes a person. Are you human only when you're born? Only when you're viable outside

Public Opinion on Overturning *Roe v. Wade*

The Supreme Court's 1973 Roe v. Wade *decision established a woman's constitutional right to an abortion, at least in the first three months of pregnancy. Would you like to see the Supreme Court completely overturn its decision or not?*

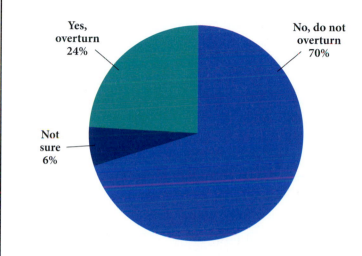

Yes, overturn 24%

No, do not overturn 70%

Not sure 6%

TAKEN FROM: NBC News/Wall Street Journal Survey, January 12–15, 2003.

of the womb? Are you less of a human life when you look like a tadpole than when you can suck on your thumb?

We're so intimidated by the wingnuts, we get spooked out of having these conversations. We let the archconservatives browbeat us with the concept of "life," using their scare tactics on women and pushing for indefensible violations like forced ultrasounds. Why? Because when they wave the not-even-accurate notion that "abortion stops a beating heart" they think they're going to trick us into some damning admission. They believe that if we call a fetus a life, they can go down the road of making abortion murder. And I think that's what concerns the hell out of those of us who support unrestricted reproductive freedom.

But we make choices about life all the time in our country. We make them about men and women in other nations. We make them about prisoners in our penal system. We make them about patients with terminal illnesses and accident victims. We still have passionate debates about the justifications of our actions as a society, but we don't have to do it while being bullied around by the vague idea that if you say we're talking about human life, then the jig is up, rights-wise.

The Life of the Mother

It seems absurd to suggest that the only thing that makes us fully human is the short ride out of some lady's vagina. That distinction may apply neatly legally, but philosophically, surely we can do better. Instead, we let right-wingers perpetuate the sentimental fiction that no one with a heart—and certainly no one who's experienced the wondrous miracle of family life—can possibly resist tiny fingers and tiny toes growing inside a woman's body. We give a platform to the notion that, as Christina Locke opined in a recent *New York Times* Op-Ed, "motherhood had slyly changed us. We went from basking in the rights that feminism had afforded us to silently pledging never to exercise them. Nice mommies don't talk about abortion."

Don't they? The majority of women who have abortions—and one in three American women will—are already mothers. And I can say anecdotally that I'm a mom who loved the lives she incubated from the moment she peed on those sticks, and is also now well over 40 and in an experimental drug trial. If by some random fluke I learned today I was pregnant, you bet your ass I'd have an abortion. I'd have the World's Greatest Abortion.

My belief that life begins at conception is mine to cling to. And if you believe that it begins at birth, or somewhere around the second trimester, or when the kid finally goes to college, that's a conversation we can have, one that I hope would be respectful and empathetic and fearless. We can't have it if those of us who believe that human life exists in utero are afraid we're somehow going to flub it for the cause. In an Op-Ed on "Why I'm Pro-Choice" in the *Michigan Daily* this week [January 22, 2013,] Emma Maniere stated, quite perfectly, that "Some argue that abortion takes lives, but I know that abortion saves lives, too." She understands that it saves lives not just in the most medically literal way, but in the roads that women who have choice then get to go down, in the possibilities for them and for their families. And I would put the life of a mother over the life of a fetus every single time—even if I still need to acknowledge my conviction that the fetus is indeed a life. A life worth sacrificing.

> *"The law is not a philosophy seminar. . . . It can take account of tragic situations without universalizing their lessons."*

Not All Abortions Are Equal

Ross Douthat

In the following viewpoint Ross Douthat argues that not all abortions occur because of dire medical circumstances, whether in the first, second, or third trimester. Douthat claims that a justification for abortion in all circumstances based on appeal to the extreme cases ignores the fact that many abortions, some quite late in pregnancy, are done for purely elective reasons. Douthat contends that the democratic process should be allowed to decide when abortion should be restricted, eliminating what he sees as a near-absolute right to abortion under any circumstances. Douthat is a columnist for the New York Times.

As you read, consider the following questions:

1. According to Douthat, abortionist George Tiller performed abortions during what trimester of pregnancy?

2. How many abortions are performed in the United States each year after the first trimester, as reported by the author?

3. Douthat argues that under current law, restrictions on abortion are only legal during what period of pregnancy?

The case of Dr. George Tiller, murdered just over a week ago in the lobby of his church, helps explain why so many people believe that abortion should be available at any stage of pregnancy.

Tiller did abortions in the third trimester, when almost no one else would do them—which meant, inevitably, that he handled the hardest of hard cases. He performed abortions on women facing life-threatening complications, on women whose children would be born dead or dying, on women who had been raped, on "women" who were really girls of 10. His Wichita, Kan., office, barricaded against protesters, was reportedly lined with thank-you notes.

Over the last week, there's been an outpouring of testimonials, across the Internet, from women (and some men) who lived through these hard cases. They help explain why Tiller thought he was doing the Lord's work, even though that work involved destroying something that we wouldn't hesitate to call a baby if we saw it struggling for life in a hospital bed. They help explain why so many Americans defend his right to do it.

But such narratives are not the only story about George Tiller's clinic. He was a target of protests—and, tragically, of terrorist violence—because he performed late-term abortions, period. But his critics were convinced that he performed them not only in truly desperate situations, but in many other cases as well. Over the years, they cobbled together a considerable amount of evidence—drawn from the state's abortion statistics, from Tiller's own comments, and from a 2006 investigation—suggesting that Tiller abused the state's mental-health exemption to justify late-term abortions in almost any situation.

This evidence is persuasive, but not dispositive. We may never know how many of George Tiller's abortions were performed on healthy mothers and healthy fetuses. But whatever the verdict on Tiller's practice, most abortions in the United States bear no resemblance whatsoever to the hardest third-trimester cases.

Yes, many pregnancies are terminated in dire medical circumstances. But these represent a tiny fraction of the million-plus abortions that take place in this country every year. (Almost half of that number are repeat abortions; around a quarter are third or fourth procedures.) The same is true of the more than 100,000 abortions that are performed after the first trimester: Very few involve medical complications of any kind. Even the now-outlawed "partial-birth" procedure, which abortion-rights supporters initially argued was only employed in the direst of dire situations, turned out to be used primarily for purely elective abortions.

The argument for unregulated abortion rests on the idea that where there are exceptions, there cannot be a rule. Because rape and incest can lead to pregnancy, because abortion can save women's lives, because babies can be born into suffering and certain death, there should be no restrictions on abortion whatsoever.

As a matter of moral philosophy, this makes a certain sense. Either a fetus has a claim to life or it doesn't. The circumstances of its conception and the state of its health shouldn't enter into the equation.

But the law is a not a philosophy seminar. It's the place where morality meets custom, and compromise, and common sense. And it can take account of tragic situations without universalizing their lessons.

Abortion Distribution Statistics

Data from the 36 areas that reported the number of previous live births for women who obtained abortions in 2009 show that 40.2%, 46.3%, and 13.6% of these women previously had zero, one to two, or three or more live births, respectively. Among the 29 reporting areas that provided these data for the relevant years of comparison, little change occurred in the distribution of abortions by the number of previous live births: the percentage of women who had zero previous live births was 39.7% in 2000 and 40.1% in 2009; the percentage of women who had one to two previous live births was 48.0% in 2000 and 46.4% in 2009; and the percentage of women who had three or more previous live births was 12.4% in 2000 and 13.5% in 2009.

Data from the 37 areas that reported the number of previous abortions for women obtaining abortions in 2009 show that the majority of women (55.3%) had not previously had an abortion; 36.6% had previously had either one to two abortions, and 8.1% had three or more abortions. Among the 30 reporting areas that provided data for the relevant years of comparison, the distribution of abortions by the number of previous abortions changed little: the percentage of women who had zero previous abortions was 55.0% in 2000 and 55.4% in 2009; the percentage of women who had one or two previous abortions was 37.3% in 2000 and 36.5% in 2009; and the percentage of women who had three or more previous abortions was 7.7% in 2000 and 8.2% in 2009.

Centers for Disease Control and Prevention,
"Abortion Surveillance—United States, 2009,"
MMWR, vol. 61, no. 8, November 23, 2012

Indeed, the argument that some abortions take place in particularly awful, particularly understandable circumstances is not a case against regulating abortion. It's the beginning of precisely the kind of reasonable distinction-making that would produce a saner, stricter legal regime.

If anything, by enshrining a near-absolute right to abortion in the Constitution, the pro-choice side has ensured that the hard cases are more controversial than they otherwise would be. One reason there's so much fierce argument about the latest of late-term abortions—Should there be a health exemption? A fetal deformity exemption? How broad should those exemptions be?—is that Americans aren't permitted to debate anything else. Under current law, if you want to restrict abortion, post-viability procedures are the only kind you're allowed to even regulate.

If abortion were returned to the democratic process, this landscape would change dramatically. Arguments about whether and how to restrict abortions in the second trimester—as many advanced democracies already do—would replace protests over the scope of third-trimester medical exemptions.

The result would be laws with more respect for human life, a culture less inflamed by a small number of tragic cases— and a political debate, God willing, unmarred by crimes like George Tiller's murder.

| *"Rape is not a moral justification for abortion."*

Abortion Is Immoral, Even in the Case of Rape or Incest

Andrew Napolitano

In the following viewpoint Andrew Napolitano argues that when pregnancy results from the crimes of rape or incest, the unborn child is innocent and has a right to life. He claims that legal abortion has resulted in mass slaughter. Furthermore, he argues that the loss of population growth from abortion has caused dire economic consequences for the country. Napolitano, a former judge of the Superior Court of New Jersey, is the senior judicial analyst at Fox News Channel and author of Theodore and Woodrow: How Two American Presidents Destroyed Constitutional Freedom.

As you read, consider the following questions:

1. The author claims that how many abortions have been performed since 1973?

2. Napolitano claims that the absence of population growth caused by abortion has resulted in what economic consequences?

3. What example does the author give of a political group that would punish a child for the crimes of his or her father?

The criticisms of the recent absurd comments by Missouri Republican Congressman Todd Akin, who at this writing [August 23, 2012,] is his party's nominee to take on incumbent Missouri Democratic Sen. Claire McCaskill in November in a contest he had been expected to win [he lost the race], have focused on his clearly erroneous understanding of the human female anatomy. In a now infamous statement, in which he used the bizarre and unheard-of phrase "legitimate rape," the congressman gave the impression that some rapes of women are not mentally or seriously resisted. This is an antediluvian [outdated] and misogynistic [woman-hating] myth for which there is no basis in fact and which has been soundly and justly condemned.

Akin also stated that the female anatomy can resist unwanted impregnation. This, too, is absurd, offensive and incorrect. Medical science has established conclusively that women cannot internally block an unwanted union of egg and sperm, no matter the relationship between male and female. I think even schoolchildren understand that.

What has gone unmentioned, however, in the cacophony of condemnation by Republicans and Democrats, is the implication in Akin's comments that rape is not a moral justification for abortion. In that, he is correct: It is not.

The Impact of Legal Abortion

Abortion takes the life of innocent human beings who are the most vulnerable in our society. Abortion is today the most frequently performed medical procedure in the United States. American physicians perform about two abortions every minute of every hour of every day: about 1 million a year since 1973. In my home state of New Jersey, abortion is permitted up to the moment of birth, and the state will even pay for it if the mother meets certain financial criteria.

How low have we sunk? What are the consequences of this mass slaughter? How did we get here?

We got here because of the most reprehensible and unconstitutional Supreme Court opinion in the modern era. In a throwback to its infamous Dred Scott decision—in which a pre–Civil War Supreme Court declared that blacks are not persons and hence cannot claim the protections of the Constitution—the court essentially said in *Roe vs. Wade* the same of fetuses in the womb.

The Absence of Population Growth

Roe vs. Wade has spawned more slaughter than all 20th-century tyrants combined. The consequences of this slaughter are vast lost generations of human beings who were denied by the law the right to live. The economic consequences from which we all suffer today—entitlements too costly to afford and too few wage earners to pay for them—are directly attributable to the absence of population growth.

I am not arguing in favor of entitlements. The Constitution does not authorize the federal government to provide them. But when FDR [former president Franklin D. Roosevelt] and LBJ [former president Lyndon B. Johnson] concocted their entitlement schemes in order to build permanent dependence on the Democratic Party, they understood population growth. Their understanding, too, was slaughtered by abortion. A society that prefers death to life not only cannot prosper; it cannot survive. Soon 40 percent of federal tax revenues will be dedicated to interest on the federal debt, and most of that borrowing has been to pay for entitlements. We are headed for a cliff.

So are the babies in the womb. But isn't the baby in a womb a person? Of course the baby in a womb is a person. The baby is produced by the physical interaction of two human parents, and every unborn baby possesses a fully actualizable human genome: all the material necessary to grow to adulthood and to exist independently outside the womb.

Abortion in Response to Rape and Incest

What about rape? Rape is among the more horrific violations of human dignity imaginable. But it is a crime committed by the male, not the female—and certainly not by the child it might produce. When rape results in pregnancy, the baby has the same right to life as any child born by mutually loving parents. Only the Nazis would punish a child for the crimes of his or her father.

Every abortion ends the life of an innocent unborn human being. When politicians in both parties claim to be pro-life but favor abortions because of the criminal behavior of the father, as in rape or incest, they are politically rejecting that hard truth. What other violations of the natural law will they condone for political expedience?

"Either we support women's right to make an abortion decision or we don't."

Respect for the Moral Agency of Women Supports Always Allowing Abortion

Ann Furedi

In the following viewpoint Ann Furedi argues that there is a moral case, as well as a pragatic one, for allowing women to make their own decisions regarding abortion throughout pregnancy. Furedi contends that attempts to draw a line in fetal development between moral abortion and immoral abortion are essentially personal judgments shrouded as rational arguments. She concludes that women should be allowed the moral autonomy to make their own private abortion decisions. Furedi is chief executive of the British Pregnancy Advisory Service, a charity in Great Britain that provides abortion counseling and treatment.

As you read, consider the following questions:

1. According to the author, Great Britain removed criminal sanctions on abortion in what year?

2. Furedi claims that in Great Britain, the number of abortions after twenty weeks remains consistent at what percentage of all abortions?

3. What technological advance does the author cite as influencing the response of society to early and late abortion?

Society's difference in attitude to early and late abortion is simple to understand on a pragmatic level. Modern democratic societies tend towards a framework of values that are relative rather than absolute. So, abortion is often perceived as 'wrong' but, at the same time, it is accepted as the 'right' thing to do *in certain circumstances*. No one likes the idea of abortion, and everyone agrees it would be better if unwanted pregnancies were prevented. But when contraception fails, or people fail to use it effectively, abortion is usually seen as preferable to the alternative: an unwanted birth to an unwilling mother. In short, abortion is a 'lesser evil'.

Public Support for Abortion

It would be difficult for society to eschew support (at least, qualified support) for abortion and maintain other values it holds dear. For example, society attaches huge importance to the wantedness of children and the responsibility that their parents have for their care. It is seen as right and proper that people should plan their families. At the same time, sex is seen as a normal, healthy part of an adult relationship: most people accept sex is an expression of love, intimacy and pleasure; no longer is it, normally, associated with the intention to reproduce. It follows from this that preventing the *conception* of unplanned, unwanted children is seen as responsible and moral.

Given that society believes that unwanted pregnancies should be prevented by contraception, it also follows that, when this fails, society accepts abortion may be used as a 'back-up' to prevent an unwanted birth.

Britain has based its law on the principle that abortion should be available to women who were 'unfit' to have children since its legislative defence against criminal abortion was codified in the Abortion Act 1967. Today, this view holds: abortion is a part of 'public health'. Almost all abortions are commissioned and funded by the state healthcare system, and access to early abortion has been part of official national strategies to improve sexual health.

But abortion still needs to be 'necessary': even at early gestations, two doctors must certify that legal grounds are met. An abortion is approved because it is the best outcome for the woman and her existing family. In essence, early abortion is justified pragmatically: it is socially necessary because, without it, the inevitable and unavoidable large numbers of unplanned pregnancies will result in the social cost of unwanted children born to unwilling mothers.

This relatively conservative rationale for abortion is accepted throughout most of society in the early weeks of pregnancy. But as the gestation advances, support for abortion declines for a combination of practical, ethical and aesthetic reasons, which are usually difficult to untangle.

The Problem of Later Abortion

There is little dispute that when abortion is necessary, there is a sound clinical case for abortion as early as possible. The risks of abortion increase with the size and development of the fetus because later abortion techniques are more specialised and are associated with a greater risk of complications. Although any increased risks associated with later abortion are still lower than those of full-term delivery, the procedure is more demanding physically and emotionally for patients and providers than in the early weeks of pregnancy.

Public support for early abortion is far stronger than for late abortion. The early abortion of an unrecognisable embryo is more acceptable to public opinion than a procedure that destroys an 'unborn baby' that is identifiably human. The ethical distinction between an abortion at six weeks and one at 16 weeks is less clear (and we will return to this point), but many hold the view that early abortion is 'more right than wrong' whereas late abortion is 'more wrong than right' and thus requires a special justification.

The pro-choice movement has tended to sidestep a moral, normative discourse, preferring to concentrate on the truthful claims that later abortions are as necessary as early abortions and so can be justified on the same grounds.

We accept that abortions should be carried out 'as early as possible'. We, too, have advocated that it is better to prevent the need for later abortions, and promote contraception. Our defence of second-trimester abortions has been based largely on the pragmatic acceptance that early abortion is not always a possible solution to a problem pregnancy and that later abortions are necessary, if regrettable. We believe that the delivery of an abortion procedure in the second (and even third) trimester is preferable to its denial, since the denial of abortion has consequences for a woman's life, for the lives that are touched by hers, and for the life of the child that will be born.

The Reasons for Later Abortions

We know that later abortions are necessary because we know why they are requested. The causes are well documented in Europe and the US, and although national circumstances affect some aspects, the reasons women give are broadly the same. In the US they tend more towards problems of access and cost, reflecting the difficulties with access and availability. In Britain, the reasons for delays are more idiosyncratic and are usually based on personal circumstances—but as research into why women have late abortions indicates, these reasons are no less compelling.

In Britain, we know that the proportion of women requesting abortions after 20 weeks remains remarkably consistent (at around two per cent) regardless of changes to access in early services. This implies that better access to early abortion would not reduce the need for later procedures. Doctors explain that there are few later abortions because women rarely request them. Many women, who would have few qualms about opting for a pregnancy to be terminated in its early weeks, balk at the thought of ending a life they have felt move inside them. A late medical induction, or a surgical procedure, is no trivial matter. . . .

If our defence of later abortion is simply as a pragmatic response to the needs of a woman with a problem pregnancy, then there is no reason to assume that any higher burden of justification is required than for earlier procedures.

If we think later abortions should only be an option in exceptional circumstances, we must ask: who should decide what those circumstances should be? And what makes a circumstance 'exceptional'? Who do we think is better placed than the woman herself to understand and judge her situation? Why do we not trust women to make the decision about whether their own circumstances are 'exceptional' enough? Do we doubt that what individuals find exceptionally compelling about their own case may be insufficiently compelling to *us*? Do we fear that others do not possess sufficient capacity to weigh the balance of 'right' and 'wrong' as precisely as we do?

This takes us into the realm of moral argument, and it is right that it should do so. We should scrutinise whether the decision to end a pregnancy is a matter for individual conscience or if it must be justified to others according to defined criteria. A discussion based on the pragmatic need for abortion does not, and cannot, address this.

The Ethics of Later Abortion

The ethical issue is straightforward for those who believe that abortion is absolutely wrong and should never be solely a matter of individual personal choice. Similarly, there is little ambiguity for those who believe that a woman has absolute autonomy to decide on the future of her pregnancy. The difficulty exists only for those who try to straddle the gap between these fundamental positions and argue that abortion should be a woman's choice, but it should be *less* of a choice in later pregnancy.

These 'ethical straddlers' represent a substantial section of the pro-choice community. Marge Berer, editor of the journal *Reproductive Health Matters*, wisely cautioned a recent pro-choice conference that: 'How late in pregnancy abortions should be permitted and carried out is a matter of great controversy among almost everyone—except the women who need them.' She might have added that even many of the 'women who need them' would claim that in general later abortion is wrong but their own case is 'exceptional'.

To me, the argument for a gradualist approach to the ethical rightness or wrongness of abortion that depends on the gestation of the fetus is weak, lacks intellectual consistency, and seems self-serving. It seems little more than an instrumental argument to justify women's access to abortion according to personal preference: to allow it when 'I approve' and to deny it when 'I don't approve'. Excepting those who think abortion is always wrong, most of us have personal preferences and subjective inclinations that cause us to empathise with some women's requests but not others'. For example, some of us will identify with the woman who requests abortion on grounds of fetal abnormality, some of us will be appalled by her thinking. Some of us will be sympathetic to a woman who wants to end a pregnancy that happened because the condom stayed in the packet; some will think her undeserving. Some of us will personally feel that an abortion is acceptable in early pregnancy, but not when more time has passed.

If we are honest, we will probably admit that we *all* make judgements about which abortions we think are right and which we think are wrong—just as women do for themselves. But there is a world of difference between making an individual judgement and seeking to constrain others from making, for themselves, the decisions we would not. Our colleagues who argue that there should be greater justification for an abortion after *x* weeks are really no different to those doctors who argue that, before they approve a woman's request, she should justify her failure to use contraception or why she is returning for a second procedure. In essence, all they are saying is that abortion should be approved when I approve and not when I do not.

The Evolving Potential of the Fetus

To the 'ethical straddlers' concerned about gestation we must ask: is there anything qualitatively different about a fetus at, say, 28 weeks that gives it a morally different status to a fetus at 18 weeks or even eight weeks? It certainly looks different because its physical development has advanced. At 28 weeks we can see it is human—at eight weeks a human embryo looks much like that of a hamster. But are we really so shallow, so fickle, as to let our view on moral worth be determined by appearance? Even if at five weeks we can only see an embryonic pole, we know that it is human. The heart that can be seen beating on an ultrasound scan at six weeks is as much a human heart as the one that beats five months later.

Claims that the fetus has 'evolving potential' make little sense. The potential of the fetus does not evolve; it just *is*. A fetus may draw closer to fulfilling this potential as it develops and as its birth approaches, but the potential does not change. Indeed, from the time of conception, as soon as embryonic cells begin to divide, an entity with the potential to become a person is created. It is the product of a man and a woman, but distinct from them. It has a unique DNA and, unless its development is interrupted or fails, it will be born as a child.

To accept that the blastocyst or embryo has the potential to evolve into a person is not to say it should be treated as a person, or even that it must be accorded moral worth because of it's potentiality. As the ethicist Professor John Harris argues, we are all potentially dead, but that does not mean that we treat people as though they are already dead.

The fact that a biological entity is potentially a person does not mean that we must treat it as a person—or even consider its moral status as special. We may wish to do this because we may feel something that has the potentiality to be a person has greater worth than something that does not. We may feel that a human embryo has greater moral status than a cat (which for all its conscious abilities and sensory perception can never be a human person), or we may believe that a cat has greater moral claims than an embryo, which is potentially a person but not yet an independent living being. Both of these positions can be presented as consistent, rational, logical arguments.

A Flawed Argument Based on Prejudice

But it is difficult to see how it can be argued that a fetus should be accorded a moral status that differs at different stages of its development on the grounds of 'evolving potential', since a fetus at 28 weeks is no more or less potentially a person than one at eight weeks.

If it is 'drawing closer' to the fulfilment of the fetus's potential that changes its moral status, then it seems that there is a difficult problem in finding a moral—as distinct from a pragmatic—justification as to when is close enough for the status to change. Since a fetus draws closer to fulfilling its potential from the day it is conceived, and is constantly evolving as it grows, which day—or which developmental change—matters morally? Is it when there is evidence of a beating heart, or fetal movement, or a particular neurological or brain development? Who makes this decision? And why?

It seems to me that the attempt to accord a 'gradualist' moral significance to the development of the fetus is little more than an attempt to disguise a personal reaction as an ethical argument. It exemplifies thinking that starts from an *a priori* [independent of experience] assumption that something is 'bad', and then tries to construct an argument to justify the badness. In this case, the assumption is that later abortions are 'bad' and the arguments about the significance of the evolving potential of the fetus are an intellectually elevated way of justifying an assumption that is, in fact, no more than prejudice.

The Appearance of the Fetus

To summarise: why should we assume later abortions are 'bad'—or, at least, 'more wrong' than early ones? There is no clinical evidence that later abortions are harmful, and certainly not more harmful than coercing an unwilling woman to endure a full-term pregnancy and labour. Later abortions are undoubtedly gruelling for both the patient and provider, but we assume that both have made a conscious decision to undertake the procedure. The life that is destroyed is no more or less a potential person than it was in early pregnancy. Late abortions may cost more and use scarce resources, but funding implications are a separate issue and distinct from the ethics of the procedure per se.

Ultimately, the distinction between early and late abortion seems reducible to our response to the appearance of the fetus—which is why so much influence has been attributed to the development of high-resolution fetal imaging, which has enabled us to see the fetus *in utero*. The argument seems reducible to this: it looks more like a child, so it should be treated more like a child.

Without doubt, it is much more difficult to countenance the destruction of a fetus once it looks like a miniature baby than before its body parts can be seen. It is even harder when an ultrasound scan shows movements that bring to mind familiar, endearing gestures—a 'yawn', thumb-sucking and grasping tiny fingers—and when we can see whether it is a boy or a girl. This is a fair enough response when it is expressed as a personal, subjective observation. It seems illegitimate, however, either dishonest or shallow, to dress it up as a moral philosophical principle.

The Moral Agency of Women

The moral principle at stake in the debate on later abortions, the one that genuinely matters, has been ignored completely in the recent discussions. This is the principle of moral autonomy in respect of reproductive decisions. To argue that a woman should no longer be able to make a moral decision about the future of her pregnancy, because 20 or 18 or 16 weeks have passed, assaults this and, in doing so, assaults the tradition of freedom of conscience that exists in modern pluralistic society. . . .

Left to make their own moral judgements, some women will inevitably make decisions that we would not; perhaps even those we think are 'wrong'. And we must live with that: tolerance is the price we pay for our freedom of conscience in a world where women can exercise their human capacity through their moral expression. We either support women's moral agency or we do not. Part of our valuing of fetal life is the value of what it means to be the humans they have the potential to become. Moral agency is part of that humanity.

The moral case for late abortion, and for preserving the right of women to exercise their moral agency in making their decision, is at least as strong as the pragmatic case. And our normative, moral case is more consistent and ploughs deeper than the instrumental attempts to find moral reasoning to restrict later abortion. Either we support women's right to make an abortion decision or we don't. We can make the judgement that their choice is wrong—but we must tolerate *their* right to decide. There is no middle ground to straddle.

| "When moral will is executed at the expense of innocent human life, I side with life—no exceptions."

The Importance of Women's Moral Will Does Not Ever Justify Elective Abortion

Karen Swallow Prior

In the following viewpoint Karen Swallow Prior argues that it is arbitrary to take the position that abortion should be allowed in some circumstances but not in others. She claims that those who consider themselves pro-life but want to allow abortion in cases of rape or incest have no consistent principle for their reasoning. Prior claims that the moral importance of innocent human life always outweighs competing reasons for abortion, including respect for the moral agency of women. Prior is a professor of English at Liberty University and a contributing writer for Christianity Today.

As you read, consider the following questions:

1. Prior claims that the attempt to demonstrate compassion by allowing abortion in the cases of rape and incest commits what two fatal errors?

2. The author notes that pro-choice activists have long held that opposition to abortion is not based on protecting life but on what?

3. Prior claims that incremental legislation, rather than outright bans on abortion, is not morally compelling but does have what benefit?

The trouble with "exceptions" on abortion—whether one is pro-life "with exceptions" or pro-choice "with exceptions"—is that exceptions make doling out abortions seem as capricious as [television show] *Seinfeld*'s Soup Nazi: "No abortion for you. Next!"

With the recent blunder of a pro-life politician hedging on the rape and abortion question, the "hard cases" in the abortion debate have gotten the pro-life movement in trouble again.

The Capriciousness of Exceptions

While well-intended (and politically prudent), the attempt to demonstrate compassion in cases of rape and incest by taking a "pro-life with exceptions" position commits the fatal errors of ignorance and inconsistency.

Consider the mental gymnastics exercised by pro-lifers uncomfortable with prohibiting abortion in cases of rape and incest: on one hand, you have those who make exceptions in such cases (thereby putting the lie to the sanctity of life claim); on the other you have those who try to make the case that pregnancies don't even occur in such cases, not the "legitimate" ones, anyway. (Note: Medically necessary abortions done to save the life of the mother are not in the same category as "elective abortions," which were made constitutional by *Roe v. Wade* [1973] and now constitute the vast majority of abortions.) Whether the "exception" is a victim of rape or incest, pregnant with a child who has an abnormality, or simply not too far along to trouble the pro-choice conscience, the result is essentially the same: a choice permitted by virtue of an arbitrary line rather than a clear, consistent principle, a la the capricious Soup Nazi. Once begun, such parsing—of abortion, of human life—can go on *ad infinitum*.

Such capriciousness, even if motivated by compassion, is inherently cruel. It generates an air of judgmentalism in deeming some situations appropriate for abortion (rape or incest) and some not (consensual sex). The implied judgment spills over like boiling soup onto all cases, even the "exceptional" ones. When even more parsing occurs to determine which cases of rape are "legitimate" and which are not, justifiable outrage only grows.

Pregnancy by Rape and Incest

Indeed, pro-choice advocates have long charged that opposing abortion is rooted more in punishing women for sexual behavior deemed immoral than in protecting human life. It's hard to argue otherwise when some claim to be pro-life but favor exceptions based not on the sanctity of life but on the sexual situation surrounding the pregnancy. Such positions, ironically, are based on choice—namely, the role that choice plays in the circumstances leading to the pregnancy.

The recent remark about "legitimate rape" may be rooted in ignorance, but such thinking did not come out of nowhere, as is widely assumed. For many years, the pro-life "Bible" was a thick little paperback by Jack Willke and his wife, Barbara, called *Abortion: Questions and Answers*. Full of factoids culled from medical journals presented in a question and answer format, the book was the go-to source for pro-life activists, myself included. It includes ten pages on the rape and incest question. The first question is, "Is pregnancy from rape common?" The answer provided is, "No. It is very rare." Several pages follow that cite dated medical research to back up this claim about what the book calls "true assault rape." So the red herring of "legitimate rape" has a long history within the pro-

Myths About Abortion

There are many myths surrounding abortion. One . . . is that all opposition to abortion is based on religious faith. A second myth is that there is a debate about "when life begins." In fact, informed parties, both those opposed to and those in favor of abortion, acknowledge that the human fetus is a living organism, growing, developing, and maintaining homeostasis. These are characteristics of living creatures. Only living things can die, and clearly the human fetus can die, so it is alive. A third myth is that the debate is about whether the "fetus is a human being." Informed participants in this discussion, regardless of their views about abortion, understand that the living organism within the woman is a member of the species *Homo sapiens*. With a human mother and a human father, with human DNA and a human path of development, the progeny is a human being. The real question in the debate is: Should all human beings be respected and protected, or just some? I favor the inclusive view in part because every single time in human history that we've chosen the exclusive view, we've made a horrible mistake.

Christopher Kaczor, interviewed by Kathryn Jean Lopez,
National Review, *October 19, 2011.*

life movement, partly because so many Americans have supported legalized abortion based on the perception that the "hard cases" are more common than they really are.

Granted, it was the pro-choice crowd that cried "rape" first, bringing before the Supreme Court a watershed abortion case falsely portrayed by its attorneys (not the woman at the center of it, Norma McCorvey, who has since become a pro-life Christian) as a rape case. Nevertheless, pro-life leaders chose to take the bait, engaging the abortion debate on those terms and spending inordinate time and energy chasing the pregnancy-as-a-result-of-rape rabbit down the hole.

A Conflict Between Two Principles

To my way of thinking, there is one compelling reason to be pro-life, and it has nothing to do with sexual morality: the inherent value of human life. This principle remains unchanged through all stages of pregnancy (and holds true in petri dishes, too). Additionally, there is one compelling reason to be pro-choice, and it has nothing to do with sexual morality: the integrity of a woman's moral will. This principle remains unchanged through all stages of pregnancy.

I see both of these principles as paramount. But with elective abortion, the two principles come into direct conflict. When moral will is executed at the expense of innocent human life, I side with life—no exceptions—life both in the abstract and in the particular lives of those who were conceived in rape. Because without life, by which I mean life in and of itself, not quality of life which, although also important, is lower on the hierarchy of needs—there cannot be a moral will. But if I weren't pro-life, I would support the integrity of a woman's moral will where it concerns her body with no exceptions as well.

Certainly, incremental pro-life legislation, rather than outright bans on abortion, may be the only approach agreeable to the massive middle, and therefore politically and practically necessary, but it doesn't fool the true believers on either side.

Not even the other side: a Christian friend of mine was once talking with a hardline feminist professor in college about the way Christians were being stereotyped throughout the class. The professor acknowledged the problem. When the conversation turned to the subject of abortion, the professor said she'd have a lot more respect for the pro-life argument without the "rape and incest" exceptions, because if human life is the principle by which one opposes abortion, then the only exceptions can be when the life of the mother is endangered.

What a pure and principled pro-life position can and should offer women with unwanted pregnancies—regardless of the circumstances of conception—is not judgment but affirmation, not the niggardly [stingy] ministerings of a Soup Nazi, but rather generous and abundant servings of the Bread of Life.

Periodical and Internet Sources Bibliography

The following articles have been selected to supplement the diverse views presented in this chapter.

Mike Adams	"Poverty, Rape, and Abortion," Townhall, July 18, 2011. www.townhall.com.
Doug Bandow	"The Consequences of the Culture of Death," *American Spectator*, June 29, 2009.
Colleen Carroll Campbell	"Abortion Proponents Distort the Meaning of Personhood," *St. Louis Post-Dispatch*, August 26, 2010.
Stuart W.G. Derbyshire	"Fetal Pain?," *Conscience*, Fall 2010.
Selwyn Duke	"Biden's Abortion Blarney," *American Thinker*, October 15, 2012. www.americanthinker.com.
Karen Espíndola	"My Body, My Choice, My Story . . ." *Women's Health Journal*, July–September 2009.
Matthew Flannagan	"Confessions of an Anti-Choice Fanatic," *Investigate*, January 2010.
Edmund C. Hurlbutt	"Abortion 'Rights' and the Duty Not to Know," *Human Life Review*, Summer 2011.
Christopher Kaczor, interviewed by Kathryn Jean Lopez	"Pro-Life Aristotle," *National Review*, October 19, 2011.
Kenneth W. Krause	"Abortion's Still Unanswered Questions," *Humanist*, July–August 2011.
Frank Pavone	"No Truce on Abortion," *Washington Times*, October 13, 2010.
Marc A. Thiessen	"Bringing Humanity Back to the Abortion Debate," *Washington Post*, April 19, 2010.

CHAPTER 2

What Has Been the Impact of *Roe v. Wade*?

Chapter Preface

The right to abortion, established in 1973 by the US Supreme Court in *Roe v. Wade*, is one of the most controversial decisions ever made by the Court. Prior to 1973, many states had laws criminalizing abortion, and in the states where abortion was allowed, it was usually only legal in very limited situations. The Court in *Roe* decided that the US Constitution guarantees a right to privacy and that this right to privacy protects a woman's right to abortion up to the point of fetal viability, the ability to live outside the uterus.

In 1965, the Supreme Court first explicitly identified a constitutional right to privacy in *Griswold v. Connecticut*. The Court held that states may not ban the sale of contraceptives—or birth control—to married couples, arguing that within the Bill of Rights there is an implicit right to marital privacy. A few years later, in 1972, the Court determined that unmarried people also have a right to privacy that protects their legal right to access and use contraceptives. These cases laid the framework for the Court's reasoning regarding the right to abortion.

The right to privacy was central to the Supreme Court's ruling in *Roe v. Wade*. Justice Harry Blackmun, who authored the Court's opinion in *Roe*, noted, "This right of privacy . . . is broad enough to encompass a woman's decision whether or not to terminate her pregnancy." The right to abortion is not absolute, however, and certain state regulation is allowed: "We . . . conclude that the right of personal privacy includes the abortion decision, but that this right is not unqualified, and must be considered against important state interests in regulation," adding that "at some point, the state interests as to protection of health, medical standards, and prenatal life, become dominant." The Court determined that because "until the end of the first trimester mortality in abortion may be less than mortality in normal childbirth," the state may impose few regulations for abortions in the first trimester. However, after the first trimester, states may regulate abortion as they regulate other medical procedures, in order to protect the health of pregnant women seeking abortions. Additionally, the Court determined that the states' interest in protecting fetal life was not relevant until viability (which it put at the beginning of the third trimester), at which point the states were permitted to disallow abortion "except when it is necessary to preserve the life or health of the mother."

In 1992, in *Planned Parenthood v. Casey*, the Court upheld the essential ruling of *Roe v. Wade* protecting a women's right to abortion in the early stages of pregnancy; however, the Court rejected the strict trimester framework of *Roe*, allowing states more freedom to regulate abortion throughout all trimesters, as long as such regulations do not pose an "undue burden" on a woman.

Today, four decades after *Roe v. Wade* established the constitutional right to abortion, the issue of abortion remains contentious. There are those who believe the Court erred in establishing a right to abortion, those who believe the decision in *Roe* was the right one, and those who believe that the Court has allowed too many restrictions on the abortion right, and there is no sign that a widespread consensus on the issue will occur anytime soon. The authors of the viewpoints in the following chapter debate this landmark ruling.

> *"The right to abort unborn children is not specifically protected by the Constitution, and prior to 1973, abortion legislation had been understood to be limited to the power of the states per the Tenth Amendment."*

Roe v. Wade Is Unconstitutional

William Sullivan

In the following viewpoint William Sullivan challenges the credibility of Roe v. Wade *(1973) and argues that it may need to be revisited in the light of new scientific progress that gives credible evidence to the notion that a fetus within a womb represents a life. Sullivan makes comparisions between slavery and abortion, claiming that they are both instances where the Supreme Court limited the rights of specific people, both the slave and unborn are not treated as a full person. Sullivan writes for* American Thinker.

As you read, consider the following questions:

1. Why does the author believe that it is unlikely that *Roe v. Wade* can be appealed?

2. According to the author, before the US Supreme Court's ruling in *Roe v. Wade*, what was the legal status of abortion in the United States?

3. What similarities are there between *Roe v. Wade* and *Dred Scott v. Sanford*, according to Sullivan?

This week, Americans celebrate, lament, or just indifferently shrug at the fortieth anniversary of that storied 7-2 decision handed down by the Supreme Court in the case of *Roe v. Wade* which legalized abortion in the United States.

A Divisive Issue

Aaron Blake of the *Washington Post* is among those shrugging his shoulders at the milestone, using the occasion to appeal to the GOP that "it's time Republicans stop talking about *Roe v. Wade.*" It's simply a lost cause, he argues, because public opinion is continually shifting to support abortion rights. "It's hard to get 70% of Americans to agree on much of anything these days," he writes. "But, for the first time, one of those things is *Roe v. Wade.*"

This conclusion that the trend we witness favors the pro-abortion crowd runs in stark contrast to the conclusion offered by *Time* magazine earlier this month. Kate Pickert offers that ever since *Roe v. Wade,* the pro-abortion lobby has lost significant ground in terms of both public opinion and legislation at the state level:

> Even though three-quarters of Americans think abortion should be legal in some or all circumstances, just 41% identified themselves as pro-choice in a Gallup survey conducted in May 2012. In this age of prenatal ultrasounds and sophisticated neonatology, a sizable majority of Americans support restrictions like waiting periods and parental consent laws. Pro-life activists write the legislation to set these rules. Their pro-choice counterparts, meanwhile, have opted to stick with their longtime core message that government should

not interfere at all with women's healthcare decisions, a stance that seems tone-deaf to the current reality.

In other words, scientific progress lends credible evidence to the notion that a fetus within a womb represents a life. Therefore, the argument that the decision to end that life is simply matter of "choice" is becoming ever more rejected by the public.

In truth, both Blake and Pickert are right. Blake is right in concluding that revisiting *Roe v. Wade* is very likely a lost cause. And Pickert is right that technological advances are undermining the narrative of the pro-abortion "power brokers" who made their push for abortion rights all those years ago. But if the pretext of "choice," which was the pivotal driver leading to *Roe v. Wade*, is increasingly rejected by the public, why is challenging the decision such a distant possibility?

There is only one possible explanation. Because leftist engineers have constructed, and because Americans generally believe, the narrative that the decision is "settled precedent," as Justice Sotomayor puts it. And because it has been so for decades, it simply doesn't matter whether the decision and its aftermath were constitutional (they weren't), whether the principle behind it is right (it isn't), or whether the decision even makes sense anymore (it doesn't).

Slavery and Abortion

Rick Santorum was on to something when he confronted Al Sharpton with the logic that "abortion is acceptable for the same reason that slavery was tolerated: both the slave and the unborn are not considered full "persons" entitled to the protection of the law." The parallel is useful here.

It is pertinent to note that the right to own slaves is not explicitly protected by the Constitution. The tenderness and divisiveness of that subject at the time of our Constitution's ratification led many of our founders to regretfully leave the issue to the discretion of the states per the Tenth Amendment.

The Trimester Reasoning in *Roe v. Wade*

1. A state criminal abortion statute . . . that excepts from criminality only a lifesaving procedure on behalf of the mother, without regard to pregnancy stage and without recognition of the other interests involved, is violative of the Due Process Clause of the Fourteenth Amendment.

2. (a) For the stage prior to approximately the end of the first trimester, the abortion decision and its effectuation must be left to the medical judgment of the pregnant woman's attending physician.

   (b) For the stage subsequent to approximately the end of the first trimester, the State, in promoting its interest in the health of the mother, may, if it chooses, regulate the abortion procedure in ways that are reasonably related to maternal health.

   (c) For the stage subsequent to viability, the State in promoting its interest in the potentiality of human life may, if it chooses, regulate, and even proscribe, abortion except where it is necessary, in appropriate medical judgment, for the preservation of the life or health of the mother.

Harry Blackmun,
Majority Opinion, US Supreme Court,
Roe v. Wade, January 22, 1973.

Many founders, however, denounced the wickedness of the slave enterprise, noted that it was contrary to the freedoms enunciated by the Declaration, and some even anticipated that the legitimacy of slavery in the context of the Constitution would be challenged by future generations. It was, and that argument was bloody, to say the least.

Slave ownership was, however, declared constitutional by Supreme Court decree, just four years before the advent of the Civil War, handed down in *Dred Scott v. Sanford*. Despite the precedent having been "settled" by this Supreme Court decision in 1857, it does not change the fact that the decision was unconstitutional, morally reprehensible, and did not make any sense at all in a time when abolitionist logic arguing for slaves' humanity and freedom was becoming increasingly accepted. As such, the decision was rightfully abrogated by the Fourteenth Amendment in 1868.

The Court's Reasoning

Likewise, the right to abort unborn children is not specifically protected by the Constitution, and prior to 1973, abortion legislation had been understood to be limited to the power of the states per the Tenth Amendment. *Roe v. Wade* introduced the specious notion that that a woman's decision, however whimsical, to abort her child is protected by a "right to privacy" guaranteed by the "due process" clause of the Fourteenth Amendment. To believe that lawmakers had abortion in mind while crafting the Fourteenth Amendment requires a Herculean leap of faith. Dissenting Justice Byron White provides the more plausible reasoning:

> I find nothing in the language or history of the Constitution to support the Court's judgment. The Court simply fashions and announces a new Constitutional right for pregnant women and, with scarcely any reason or authority for its action, invests that right with sufficient substance to override most existing state abortion statutes.

Roe v. Wade not only established abortion (for any chosen reason) as constitutional under curious pretenses, but it functioned as a federal edict granting new powers to the federal government—the power to provide an eternal allowance for abortion under the newly created guidelines prescribed by the ruling. And these guidelines and timetables by which states can legally proscribe abortion (the particulars of which were clearly not included in the Fourteenth Amendment) were arbitrarily decided upon by the Court, not federal lawmakers. In spite of this seemingly egregious usurpation of the powers of the legislative branch by the judiciary, the ruling in its entirety is now somehow understood to function as law.

So under the pretense of "privacy" and "choice" and without convincing legislative grounding, wholesale abortion became allowable by federal authority. The decision only passively entertains the notion of the unborn life's humanity that is increasingly understood today, ruling that states can have some flexibility in deeming the life "viable" and protecting it in certain conditions after the first trimester—but never before.

Roe v. Wade Is Unconstitutional

So yes, *Roe v. Wade* and its application can be convincingly described as unconstitutional. Abortion can be as morally reprehensible as murder if modern science is to be believed. And the decision's underlying principle of "choice" is being increasingly rejected by the public. But despite all of this, and despite the overwhelming support to curtail frivolous abortion at the state level in recent years, it's untouchable.

I don't necessarily argue against the conclusion that it would be a political mistake for Republicans to target *Roe v. Wade*. But if hindsight is truly 20/20, and in light of what we can now reasonably know to be the truth about the flaws in *Roe v. Wade*'s genesis and legacy that surpasses holocaustic magnitude, the pressing question we need to ask of our society is: Why?

> *"The actual text—in the Ninth Amendment and the [Fourteenth Amendment's] Privileges or Immunities Clause—provides a sound basis for the recognition of rights that are not expressly mentioned [in the Constitution]."*

Roe v. Wade Is Not Unconstitutional

Michael C. Dorf

In the following viewpoint Michael C. Dorf disputes three criticisms of the US Supreme Court's decision in Roe v. Wade *(1973). First, Dorf denies that because the US Constitution never uses the word* abortion *there is no constitutional protection for abortion. Second, Dorf denies that a constitutional defense of abortion rests on the confirmation that the authors of the Constitution meant to protect abortion. Finally, he denies that the Court ought to stay out of controversial issues. Dorf is the Robert S. Stevens Professor of Law at Cornell University Law School and a columnist for the legal news website Justia.com.*

As you read, consider the following questions:

1. Dorf suggests that the language of which amendment to the US Constitution best encompasses the right to abortion?

2. According to the author, how extensive was regulation of abortion at the time the Fourteenth Amendment was adopted?

3. What is one of the three examples the author gives where the US Supreme Court failed to stand up for constitutional rights?

Tuesday, January 22, 2013, will mark the fortieth anniversary of *Roe v. Wade*, the Supreme Court ruling that recognized a constitutional right of a woman to have an abortion. What lessons can we learn from the case and the ensuing years?. . .

I consider three common criticisms of the ruling: (1) that the constitutional text nowhere mentions abortion; (2) that the original meaning of the Fourteenth Amendment did not encompass a right to abortion; and (3) that the courts ought to stay out of socially divisive issues.

I explain why the arguments based on each of these claims are misguided and potentially dangerously so: Misunderstanding what made *Roe* a controversial case may mislead lawyers and Supreme Court Justices in their thinking about other controversial social questions, like those raised about same-sex marriage in the cases now pending before the high Court. . . .

One: The Constitution Does Not Mention Abortion

Critics of *Roe* sometimes say that the Constitution does not mention abortion, and that therefore the regulation of abortion is left to the political process. Yet the Constitution does not—in so many words—mention other rights that we take for granted as encompassed within the general language of broader provisions.

For example, the Constitution does not specifically mention movies but the courts have little difficulty seeing them as protected by the First Amendment. Likewise, the Equal Protection Clause of the Fourteenth Amendment does not use the words "race," "sex" or "religion," but courts rightly invalidate most laws discriminating on those grounds.

So, what general language encompasses the right to abortion? The best textual answer would point to the Ninth Amendment, which says: "The enumeration in the Constitution, of certain rights, shall not be construed to deny or disparage others retained by the people." Under the most straightforward reading, that language says that there are unenumerated rights that limit the federal government. Moreover, a provision of the Fourteenth Amendment tells state governments that they may not "make or enforce any law which shall abridge the privileges or immunities of citizens of the United States," which, under a similarly straightforward reading, binds the state governments to respect the same rights, including the unenumerated rights, that limit the federal government.

For historical reasons, however, the Supreme Court did not locate the abortion right in the Ninth Amendment or the Privileges or Immunities Clause. Instead, the Court in *Roe* held that the "liberty" encompassed by the Due Process Clauses of the Fifth and Fourteenth Amendments includes the freedom to choose to have an abortion prior to fetal viability.

Sticklers have long objected to the doctrine of "substantive due process" that was used in *Roe*, but their real quarrel is with the Court, rather than the Constitution. The actual text—in the Ninth Amendment and the Privileges or Immunities Clause—provides a sound basis for the recognition of rights that are not expressly mentioned.

Thus, critics of *Roe* who invoke the Constitution's supposed silence on abortion must be prepared to jettison much more than abortion rights. The Court found an unenumerated right of married couples to use contraception in 1965 in *Griswold v. Connecticut*. Must that right also go? And if the failure of the Constitution to use the word "abortion" means that *Roe* is wrong, then there would also be no constitutional basis for resisting a law that *required* a woman to have an abortion. The pro-lifers who denounce *Roe* cannot be happy with that consequence.

Two: The Original Meaning of the Fourteenth Amendment

Another critique of *Roe* asserts that it fails to respect the original understanding of the Fifth Amendment (ratified in 1791) or the Fourteenth Amendment (ratified in 1868). This argument rests on the false premise that contemporary constitutional rights must be grounded in original understanding, narrowly understood. . . .

Very few scholars or judges who call themselves "originalists" consider themselves bound by the subjective intentions and expectations of the people who proposed and ratified the Constitution and its amendments. Those intentions and expectations are often unknowable, and even to the extent that they can be known, they were not enacted. Only the text was enacted—and as we have seen, the text is sufficiently capacious to encompass unenumerated rights. Once the courts are in the business of finding which aspects of "liberty" receive constitutional protection, it hardly seems unreasonable to conclude that women have a right against the government conscripting their bodies to serve as involuntary incubators for nine months.

Moreover, Justice Harry Blackmun's majority opinion in *Roe* is actually more attentive to original understanding than are many constitutional rulings that we accept as clearly legiti-

The Right to Privacy in the US Constitution

Specific guarantees in the Bill of Rights have penumbras, formed by emanations from those guarantees that help give them life and substance. Various guarantees create zones of privacy. The right of association contained in the penumbra of the First Amendment is one. . . . The Third Amendment, in its prohibition against the quartering of soldiers "in any house" in time of peace without the consent of the owner, is another facet of that privacy. The Fourth Amendment explicitly affirms the "right of the people to be secure in their persons, houses, papers, and effects, against unreasonable searches and seizures." The Fifth Amendment, in its Self-Incrimination Clause, enables the citizen to create a zone of privacy which government may not force him to surrender to his detriment. The Ninth Amendment provides: "The enumeration in the Constitution, of certain rights, shall not be construed to deny or disparage others retained by the people."

William O. Douglas,
majority opinion, US Supreme Court,
Griswold v. Connecticut, June 7, 1965.

mate. The Court in *Roe* addresses the legal treatment of abortion throughout history, from ancient times, through medieval England, in colonial and Founding-Era America, and on into the Nineteenth and Twentieth Centuries. From this history, the Court concludes that certainly at the Founding, and even by the time that the Fourteenth Amendment was adopted, abortion was subject to less restrictive regulation than was the case in 1973, when *Roe* was handed down. Although that point does not show that the original understanding of the Fifth and Fourteenth Amendments necessarily protected a right to abortion, it does tend to show that an abortion right is consistent with original understanding.

Three: The Courts Should Stay Out of Socially Divisive Issues

A third line of criticism says that the *Roe* Court erred by taking sides in a divisive social controversy. Critics sometimes analogize [compare] *Roe* to *Dred Scott v. Sandford* [1856], which declared African Americans ineligible for citizenship and helped precipitate the Civil War. But that analogy hardly supports the view that the Court ought to stay out of divisive controversies. From a modern perspective, the problem with the *Dred Scott* ruling is not that the Court took sides on the question of slavery in the territories, but that it took the wrong side.

We tend to lionize the Supreme Court when it ends up on the right side of history. The Court's 1954 ruling invalidating de jure [legalized] racial segregation in *Brown v. Board of Education* is now widely regarded as its finest hour. Yet, as [journalist] Linda Greenhouse reminds us in a recent discussion of the late [disapproved Supreme Court nominee] Robert Bork's career, in its day and for over a decade thereafter, *Brown* was highly controversial. Under the *Roe* critics' reasoning, that means *Brown* too was wrongly decided.

American constitutional history is messy. A controversial ruling may spark a backlash against the cause it embraces. Or it may serve as a moral beacon and a catalyst for an emerging movement to triumph on the field of social and political contestation.

With no crystal ball, judges should be cautious in recognizing previously unheralded rights, but not to the point of abdicating their responsibility. For while the Court has sometimes erred by invoking the Constitution to lead where the

People do not wish to follow, it has also erred by shirking its duty to stand up for constitutional rights—as it did with respect to Jim Crow [segregation laws] for the nearly six decades between *Plessy v. Ferguson* [1896] and *Brown*; during the Red Scare [fear of communism] of the First World War and again during McCarthyism [another Red Scare promoted by US senator Joseph McCarthy in the 1950s]; and when it accepted the military's forced evacuation of Japanese Americans during World War II in *Korematsu v. United States* [1943]. These were examples of the Court's failing because it refused to enter a divisive controversy.

Why *Roe* Was a Hard Case

Accordingly, the three criticisms I have highlighted do not identify a problem with *Roe*—or if they do, they also identify a problem with numerous Supreme Court cases having nothing to do with abortion.

Roe was nonetheless a difficult case, because an unwanted pregnancy pits two very important interests against one another: the interest in the life or potential life of a fetus versus the freedom of a woman to control her own body. No legal resolution to that conflict will satisfy everyone, regardless of whether a legislature, a court, or an individual woman resolves it.

The ongoing controversy concerning *Roe* is a product of the high stakes from both sides' vantage points, and the place where American public opinion has come uneasily to rest.

> *"By 2011 more than half of all US women of reproductive age were living in states deemed hostile to abortion rights."*

Roe v. Wade Has Not Removed the Challenges to Obtaining an Abortion

Eleanor J. Bader

In the following viewpoint Eleanor J. Bader argues that anti-abortion protesters and anti-abortion legislation is increasingly making it more difficult for women to obtain an abortion. Bader asserts that the number of abortion clinics has declined in recent years and that many American women live in areas where there is no abortion provider. She contends that legislation around the country targets poor women and minors, adding obstacles to accessing the legal right to abortion. Bader is a teacher at Kingsborough Community College and the Pratt Institute, both in New York City, and is coauthor of Targets of Hatred: Anti-abortion Terrorism.

Eleanor J. Bader, "Forty Years After *Roe v. Wade*, Getting an Abortion Is Still a Major Challenge," *On the Issues*, Winter 2013. Copyright © 2013 by Eleanor J. Bader. All rights reserved. Reproduced by permission.

As you read, consider the following questions:

1. What fraction of American women will have had an abortion by the age of forty-five, according to the author?

2. How many states, according to Bader, allow low-income women to use Medicaid to pay for an abortion without restrictions?

3. What are TRAP laws, according to Bader?

Ramona, 32, mother of a four-year-old daughter, is dropped off at the Summit Women's Center in Bridgeport Connecticut at 8 a.m. on a frigid December Saturday. As she gets out of the car to walk the thirty feet to the clinic, she notices a dozen people holding weathered pictures of mangled babies bearing the words "abortion kills." The protesters can't trespass on clinic property or enter the fenced-in parking lot, but plastic bullhorns amplify their voices. "The Lord loves you," they shout. "He has a purpose for every life. You don't need to go in there and murder your child."

"I didn't want to be rude so I approached them when they called out to me," says Ramona, once inside the clinic. (All quotes are verbatim; name has been changed to protect privacy). "They bombarded me. They said that if I go through with the abortion I'll become so depressed that I'll start to drink and do drugs and will think about suicide."

"I was dropped off this morning by my mom," she continued. "My little girl was also in the car and I don't know what she understood or heard. These people say they want to help me, but how does traumatizing my child help me? They've made my life harder because now I have to worry about whether she heard them, saw the pictures they were carrying, or is scared because she heard people yelling at her mommy."

As she speaks, Ramona's voice rises with indignation and fury. "I know that this is not the right time for me to have a second child. I've discussed the pregnancy with my family and with my personal physician and I know I'm doing the right thing, the best thing, for all of us. How can these strangers think they know better?"

The Rise in Anti-Abortion Protests

Good question. Forty years after the Supreme Court's *Roe v. Wade* decision was issued, the idea that abortion may at times be the best option for women and families remains contentious. True, great advances in the availability of safe abortion care have been made since 1973. But the vigilance of anti-abortion protests has also ramped up.

Members of the Connecticut chapter of the North Carolina–based Operation to Save America (OSA) are a frequent presence outside the Summit Women's Center in Bridgeport. And while regular picket lines, like this one, are fewer and farther between than they were 25 years ago, OSA continues to conduct "sidewalk counseling" in many cities throughout the United States. Ringleader Marilyn Carroll, the head of the state's OSA chapter, is at the Summit Women's Center when Ramona is accosted.

Fortunately, once Ramona is inside Summit the atmosphere changes. The Center, which opened in 1975 and is now owned by David Lipton, is located on Bridgeport's Main Street. Its ambiance is pleasant and inspiring signs decorate the walls:

> The staff in this office does sacred work and though you may hope to never come back, we return each day to hear your stories, hold your hands, and ease your fears. Our lives are consumed with caring for yours. In these walls and in our hearts you are forever valued, treasured, respected and safe.

Despite being rattled by the antis, Ramona's decision to have an abortion is ironclad. Indeed, the presence of the antis has done little to stop women from terminating unwanted

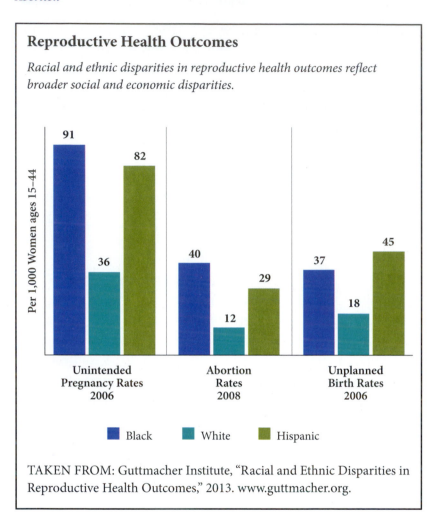

Reproductive Health Outcomes

Racial and ethnic disparities in reproductive health outcomes reflect broader social and economic disparities.

Per 1,000 Women ages 15–44

	Unintended Pregnancy Rates 2006	Abortion Rates 2008	Unplanned Birth Rates 2006
Black	91	40	37
White	36	12	18
Hispanic	82	29	45

■ Black   ■ White   ■ Hispanic

TAKEN FROM: Guttmacher Institute, "Racial and Ethnic Disparities in Reproductive Health Outcomes," 2013. www.guttmacher.org.

pregnancies. According to the Guttmacher Institute, nearly one-third of U.S. women will have an abortion by the time they turn 45. Ninety percent will end these unwanted pregnancies—either medically or surgically—during the first trimester. Like Ramona, 61 percent already have at least one child at the time of their abortion.

A Decline in the Number of Clinics

At the same time, Guttmacher notes that the current number of annual terminations is lower than it was a decade ago. Still, more than one million abortions a year continue to be performed, and given the frequency of the procedure, it would not be far-fetched to imagine abortion facilities being as ubiquitous as nail salons or dental offices. But they aren't. In fact, five states—Arkansas, Mississippi, North Dakota, South Dakota and Wyoming—have just one provider, and OSA head Flip Benham has publicly declared that he intends to turn these states into "anti-abortion refuges."

Guttmacher confirms that the number of clinics has shrunk, from approximately 2,500 in the early 1980s to less than 1,800 today. While the reasons for this reduction are complex, at least part of the decline rests with the anti-abortion movement's relentless crusade to malign the procedure. Popular culture has also played a role. Television is replete with constant just-in-the-nick-of-time miscarriages—with the notable exception of one episode of *Friday Night Lights* several years back—keeping abortion off the small screen. The big screen is no better. In the Academy Award–winning film *Juno*, to cite just one example, a young teenager contemplates having an abortion—that is, until she enters a drab clinic where healthcare is dispensed by a callous and uncaring staff.

Combine this with the efforts of state legislators who want to make a name for themselves by pandering to the religious and secular rightwing, and the upshot, Guttmacher reports, is that by 2011 more than half of all US women of reproductive age were living in states deemed hostile to abortion rights. Among the many roadblocks: Only 17 states currently allow Medicaid to pay for the abortions of low-income women. The remaining 33 allow Medicaid to be used only if the pregnancy is the result of rape or incest or would likely result in death if carried to term.

The Targeting of Minors

Poor women are not the only targets: Thirty-seven states require parental involvement when a minor wants an abortion—the consent or notification of one or both parents/guardians or a judge in cases in which parental involvement is impossible or is counter-indicated. Seventeen states require a 24-to-72-hour waiting period between pre-abortion counseling—which frequently includes the well-refuted link between abortion and breast cancer—and the procedure, and 18 states bar "partial birth" abortions, a specific and once-rare late-term surgery. In addition, five states—Alabama, Idaho, Indiana, Kansas and Oklahoma—ban abortion after 20 weeks, a restriction pushed by antis who charge that fetuses older than 20 weeks feel pain, something that is impossible to know. What's more, seven states [Arizona, Kansas, Nebraska, North Dakota, South Dakota, Oklahoma, and Tennessee] ban telemedical conferencing for medication abortions. In these locales, patients must come into a clinic, in person, before a prescription can be issued, posing an often-severe hardship for the underserved rural women that telemedicine was established to help.

And lest you wonder how and why state after state passes similar restrictions, the answer lies with Americans United for Life [AUL], an anti-choice organization that has crafted 32 pieces of model legislation that are peddled to law makers interested in limiting abortion access. Their well-honed message has gained a toehold in political life and in outreach to people of color: AUL insists that abortion and birth control are part of a Caucasian plot to annihilate people of color and limit the growth of future generations.

Anti-abortion materials also target young people: Pamphlets such as "This is Not Your Only Choice," created by the Human Life Alliance, are left in medical waiting rooms, community centers and public and parochial schools—and posted online and on social networking sites. They plant the idea that abortion is physically and psychologically damaging.

"When I discovered I was pregnant I felt desperately alone. I cried myself to sleep," the brochure begins. "I decided to confide in a couple of college professors who collected money to fly me out of town to have an abortion. Now I felt obligated to go through with it. Still, I agonized. I was summoned to the room where the abortions were being performed. I could hear a woman sobbing in the recovery room. That memory still haunts me." The pamphlet then describes a change of heart and the subsequent birth of a child who is loved and cherished. Then—surprise—this woman's story is juxtaposed with that of another woman, and the second tale is replete with uncontrollable depression, anxiety and regret—all of it caused, you guessed it, by the abortion. A section called "After-Abortion Trauma" hammers the message and in case you missed the point, everything from eating disorders to suicidal ideation is attributed to the termination. If you don't know better, it's scary stuff.

The Defense of Abortion Providers

Needless to say, the relentless attacks on the efficacy of abortion and the incremental chipping away at abortion availability—to say nothing of the murder and wounding of 20 clinic staffers since 1993—have infuriated providers of reproductive healthcare, feminists, and prochoice activists. Worse, the constant attacks have kept these constituencies scrambling, constantly working to defeat the onslaught of anti-choice legislation on the state and federal levels. At the same time they've labored to undo the stigma that has taken hold.

Prochoice organizing—demonstrating, lobbying, and doing clinic defense and post-abortion counseling—has kept reproductive health advocates extremely busy, trying to hold access steady and fight incursions on who can have an abortion and when they can have it. It's been an uphill struggle. In addition to trying to ensure patient and staff safety, providers in several states have also had to fend off a host of indirect attacks promulgated by anti-choice forces, including boycotts and pickets of suppliers, rental agents, delivery services and construction crews. Arkansas' Little Rock Family Planning, for example, was informed last winter that the oxygen and nitrous oxide supplier they'd used for 15 years was suspending deliveries because the antis had brought them negative publicity. Although the clinic was able to find another provider, staff had to spend valuable time making new arrangements.

The antis hope that creating distractions and extra work for clinicians will drive them out of the field, says Charlotte Taft, the director of the Abortion Care Network [ACN], an organization of independent abortion and reproductive health care providers. In Texas, she says, anyone can file an anonymous complaint with the state health department or environmental control board and it will be investigated. "Every single time a complaint is filed an inspector comes to the clinics and casts doubt on them. The antis then use the fact that an inspector showed up as a recruitment tool, saying, 'See, the conditions here are so awful that the inspectors had to come out and check everything again.'" Taft calls it harassment and admits that the near-constant scrutiny makes it difficult for providers to do their jobs.

Likewise TRAP laws, short for Targeted Regulation of Abortion Providers[, make it difficult for providers]. Taft charges that such laws are often unnecessary and, more often than not, require clinics to become ambulatory surgical centers. "One of the ACN clinics in Pennsylvania has been renting an office space for the past 20 years but thanks to passage of a TRAP law, they've been told that they need to enlarge their hallways by four inches. They don't own the building and there is no logical reason for them to have to do this. At a time when everyone's money is tight, if they have to reconstruct the facility it will drive up the cost of health care." That's not even the worst of it, Taft continues. "The most appalling thing is that widening the halls will do absolutely nothing to improve the safety of this already extremely safe medical procedure."

Laws Purportedly Based on Safety

The illusion of improving safety is also at the heart of a spate of newly introduced bills to require abortion providers to have admitting privileges at local hospitals. On the face of it, it sounds sane. After all, if you have an abortion in St. Paul, Minnesota, doesn't it stand to reason that your doctor should be able to have you admitted to a specific St. Paul hospital, rather than send you to an Emergency Room, should complications arise? What the requirement fails to acknowledge, prochoice experts argue, is that abortion patients almost never need to be hospitalized. Secondly, since clinics typically employ doctors from out of town, most hospitals are leery of granting privileges to someone who is present only once or twice a week.

The Volunteer Women's Medical Clinic in Knoxville, Tennessee is a case in point. Thanks to state passage of The Life Defense Act, the 38-year-old facility had to be shuttered in August after its longtime physician, a man who had local admitting privileges, passed away and his replacement was unable to obtain them. The closure likely cheered abortion foes who are relentlessly pursuing a campaign to close each and every abortion facility in the country. The delusion, says ACN's Charlotte Taft, is that closing abortion facilities will end abortion.

"Before *Roe* women who needed abortions were willing to get into a strange car, be blindfolded, pay the equivalent of thousands of dollars, and not know where they were going or who was going to perform their surgery. Even though it was hard for women to find abortionists, they did what they had to do. Abortion comes from women's sense of responsibility, and it is important to understand that roadblocks to abortion don't stop them."

Want to be truly prolife? Taft asks. Then support comprehensive sex education, childcare, equal wages for women and accessible and affordable birth control.

Indeed, staff at Bridgeport, Connecticut's Summit Women's Center point out that if the antis cared about women's lives as much as they say they do, they would move their protests far from clinic entrances. "Having the antis out front is horrible for our patients," says clinic administrator Tanya Little, a staffer since 1999. "It's also horrible for those of us who work here. Some days I find it difficult to restrain myself from talking back. On the other hand, seeing the protesters every day reaffirms my dedication to do this work because who are they to tell anyone else what to do? I feel good about providing women with options and supporting them in whatever choice they make, whether it's childbirth, adoption, or termination. Our entire staff is adamant that we are going to continue and not be afraid or bullied."

> *"The abortion argument rages because from the beginning it's been hijacked by absolutists even as [the] public . . . gives every evidence of being somewhere between the two extremes."*

Roe v. Wade Launched a Debate of Absolutists That Ignores the Majority

Steve Erickson

In the following viewpoint Steve Erickson argues that since the US Supreme Court's decision in Roe v. Wade *(1973), the abortion debate has been dominated by extremists. Erickson contends that the pro-life side is overly rigid about its rejection of abortion in any circumstance, whereas the pro-choice side is overly rigid in its failure to accept any restrictions on abortion. Erickson suggests a compromise that recognizes the inherent moral conundrum and allows unrestricted abortion only during the first half of pregnancy, without any government funding. Erickson is a writer and teacher at the California Institute of the Arts.*

As you read, consider the following questions:

1. What two analogies does the author use to support his view that just because the Constitution guarantees the right to abortion does not mean government should subsidize it?

2. Erickson claims that the pro-choice movement appeals to what kind of faulty slippery-slope logic regarding abortion?

3. Erickson suggests that the US Supreme Court should move the demarcation line of viability for regulating abortion to how many weeks?

Forty years after the Supreme Court found a constitutional right to abortion [in 1973] in the Fourth Amendment on behalf of "Jane Roe"—a 25-year-old single mother in Texas named Norma McCorvey—America is as unsettled as ever on the issue. This is for two reasons that, by their nature, are at odds with each other. The first is that abortion is a metaphysical enigma to which neither wisdom nor experience provides a definitive answer; we're therefore left to fashion an imperfect political response to a question that's fundamentally spiritual. The second is that, as with other more banal political matters these days, into the vacuum of what human beings can know about the soul rush ideological extremes that concede nothing to ambiguity let alone another point of view.

The Court's Decision

At the center of the dilemma over terminating a pregnancy is this consideration: At what point does a biological entity initially part of a woman's body cross into the realm of its own humanity? Merely asking this is anathema to those opposed to abortion under any circumstances, because thinking independently about such things is anathema to religious orthodoxy which doesn't allow for the possibility that the fetus ever is something unto the woman. Conversely, trucking in the vocabulary of metaphysics and fetal extermination unsettles those who believe most fiercely in a woman's right to an abortion because it allows for the possibility that infanticide might ever be involved. The abortion argument rages because from the beginning it's been hijacked by absolutists even as a public so uncomfortable with abortion that it can't bear to discuss it gives every evidence of being somewhere between the two extremes.

Conservatives are right about *Roe v. Wade.* To extrapolate from the Fourth Amendment's protection against search and seizure a right to privacy was reasonable; to extrapolate from a right to privacy a constitutional right to an abortion was extraordinary. This isn't to say that the freedom to have an abortion isn't worth formulating. Many freedoms aren't expressly established by the Bill of Rights, which is why the Ninth Amendment states that the government can't presume an individual right doesn't exist simply because it isn't so established. It is to say that *Roe v. Wade* had less to do with legal logic than with what liberals at the time considered the political necessity of putting the Constitution on the side of abortion—something about which even progressive scholars like Laurence Tribe and Alan Dershowitz, columnist Michael Kinsley, and Justice Ruth Bader Ginsburg have expressed skepticism down through the years. Out of the original flawed decision grew flawed extending arguments, the most specious of which (before it became part of the more recent conversation about health-care reform) committed the government to subsidizing abortions for those women who can't afford them in order that they're "guaranteed" their constitutional freedom. It could well be that the government should subsidize abortions for poor women if there's a national consensus to do so. But the First Amendment that recognizes a man's right to a free press doesn't obligate the government to buy him a newspaper, a laptop, or a pencil, and the Second Amendment that recognizes a man's right to bear arms doesn't obligate the government to buy him a gun.

The Absolutism of Both Sides

For much of the last 40 years, the pro-choice movement's political victories undercut its moral authority, which reached a nadir in the 1990s with the controversy over late-term or "partial birth" abortions. Having lost confidence in its ability to mount a medical case let alone a moral one, the movement reflexively fell back on the slippery-slope contention that has come to vex so much political logic, which is that to ban late-term abortions inevitably opens the door to banning all abortion (the National Rifle Association makes a similar argument against gun regulation). This contention only reinforces the dynamic that's framed a 40-year debate by which we either outlaw all abortion beginning at the moment of conception or permit all abortion up until the moment of birth.

Whether the absolutism of one extreme answered or precipitated the absolutism of the other now matters as little as the original soundness of *Roe v. Wade* itself. Constitutional freedom always has been evolutionary notwithstanding the insistence of strict constructionists who know nothing about the document or about those who wrote and debated it; two generations of women after *Roe v. Wade*, the right to an abortion now is encoded in the genetics of freedom. In the meantime the intellectual bankruptcy of the pro-choice movement has been matched by a meanness that characterizes a pro-life movement often led and voiced by the gender that never has babies (and sometimes writes articles like this). The pro-life movement's essential problem is with the nature of democracy, which not only accepts but insists that no one is ever completely right or wrong and that in this fact lies resolutions born of compromise. Metastasizing into something hard and ungenerous (and un-Christian) enough to make stupefying statements about rape, at its core much of the pro-life movement isn't about saving fetuses. At its core, as codified by the unforgiving platform of the Republican Convention last summer [in 2012], much of the pro-life movement is about middle-aged men punishing young women for having sex.

A Proposed Middle Ground

Should we assume there's an answer to when the life of the soul begins, nonetheless—barring some visitation of divine insight more convincing than the one to which religious people lay claim and which God has chosen to deny the rest of us—that answer remains unknowable. Before the Supreme Court interceded to declare the constitutionality of abortion, a national plebiscite [referendum] on abortion rights in which only women could vote would have been ideal, but we don't submit constitutional rights to plebiscites, so those disinclined to join one camp or the other at one far end or the other of the debate are left to forge an uneasy consensus. Notwithstanding the fallacies of *Roe v. Wade*, the law has been "settled" too long now to be overturned; conservative justices William Rehnquist and Sandra Day O'Connor implicitly acknowledged this 20 years ago. The decision's stipulation of 24 weeks as the point at which a fetus becomes "viable," however, has been rendered obsolete by technology; babies are born earlier and surviving. Rather than leave the concept of viability to individual states, which is an invitation to chaos, the Court should revisit it, moving the demarcation line back to 19 weeks, half of what's considered by modern medicine a normal 38-week pregnancy. Unless the national mood changes, the federal government shouldn't be financing abortions. Subsidization undercuts the argument that abortion should be an individual choice and therefore an individual responsibility made and assumed by the individual woman; abortion is too incendiary for too many millions of sincere, pro-life Americans who shouldn't have the power to impose their beliefs on a pregnant woman but who by the same token shouldn't have to pay for her abortion. While we all pay taxes for things we don't believe in, such as bad wars, war isn't something that individuals declare on their own. On the other hand, if the government's refusal to pay for abortions isn't a denial of constitutional freedom, then the concerted effort by state and local governments to make access to abortion impossible is, as is happening in Mississippi, Arkansas, and North and South Dakota. Those states should cease and desist their schemes to target and eliminate family-planning clinics or be sued by the Justice Department.

The only people who will find the above controversial are those who fight over abortion the hardest and whose rhetoric has long since exchanged light for heat. Those who believe a fertilized egg is fully a human being will reject any middle-ground that includes what can only be murder in their minds. But although in a totalitarian state—where mind-control is the order of the day—an intense spirituality collectively shared by many people can become a blow for freedom because it reaches deeper than the mind to where neither police nor government can go, in a democracy that exalts tolerance the political outcome of single-mindedness is anarchy or authoritarianism. This spirituality is hostile to moral nuance and determined to cast all issues in terms that don't allow for the commonality from which pluralistic nations are built.

Maybe this national characteristic is borne out of a frontier mentality that couldn't help but view existence in brutal life-and-death terms. Maybe it goes back farther to the colonization of the land by religious fanatics, at once persecuted and persecuting. In any case the squeamish middle needs to seize control of this quarrel so as to decide for a nation at large something that never can be decided by the quarrelers. While the mandate of religion is to banish doubt, the mandate of politics is to accommodate it, and those of us not so presumptuous to think we understand the soul's machinery or how or when the off-on switch gets flipped are left to make the best we can of the darkness. We're left to strike a humane balance among those to whom we extend the benefit of the doubt when extremists defy doubt itself. Neither playing nor denying God, we navigate that moment when doubt's benefit on behalf of the mother accedes to that of the fetus and a decision to abort is resolved at the nexus of maternal conscience, medical circumstance, and the murmurs of a Creator we can barely hear.

> "Roe *may matter less than many people realize—or perhaps matter for different reasons than commonly thought."*

Does *Roe* Still Matter?

Daniel Allott

In the following viewpoint Daniel Allott argues that there are misconceptions about how the US Supreme Court's decision in Roe v. Wade *(1973) impacts the legality of abortion. If* Roe *was overturned, Allott claims, not much would change with respect to the availability of abortion in the states. Despite this, Allott notes that there is a symbolic significance to* Roe *and, for this reason, both the pro-life and pro-choice factions believe* Roe *is important, with the former wanting it overturned and the latter wanting it to remain the law of the land. Allott is a writer in Washington, DC.*

As you read, consider the following questions:

1. What mistaken belief does the author claim most people have about what would happen if *Roe v. Wade* was overturned?

2. What percentage of pregnant South Dakota women had abortions in 2008, and what was the national average, as reported by Allott?

3. Allot claims the Center for Reproductive Rights estimates that how many states would protect abortion fully even if *Roe* were overturned?

Earlier this week [in late January 2012], abortion and pro-life advocates observed the 39th anniversary of the Supreme Court's *Roe v. Wade* decision, which, along with its companion case, *Doe v. Bolton*, recognized abortion to be a constitutionally protected right while giving states some leeway in restricting its availability.

Roe dominates America's abortion debate. If you had asked any of the scores of thousands of pro-lifers who poured into Washington, D.C., on Monday for the annual March for Life to name their most urgent priority, most would have said overturning *Roe*.

Abortion advocates, meanwhile, talk about *Roe* as if it were the only thing standing between women and a new era of back alley abortions. As NARAL Pro-Choice America states on its website, "We believe that women should have the option to choose abortion. Today they can, thanks to the Supreme Court's *Roe v. Wade* decision in 1973."

But *Roe* may matter less than many people realize—or perhaps matter for different reasons than commonly thought. Many people mistakenly believe that legal abortion hinges on *Roe*—that without *Roe* abortion would be illegal everywhere in America. But that's not true. If *Roe* goes, abortion law would revert to the states to decide.

Others mistakenly believe that the number of abortions would drop precipitously if *Roe* goes. That likely would not happen. Consider how abortion is treated in two states: South Dakota and California.

Relatively few abortions take place in South Dakota because South Dakotans are generally pro-life and elect pro-life lawmakers who have passed a number of restrictions on abortion. They include parental notification laws, bans on public funding of abortion and a requirement that women seeking abortion be given pro-life counseling.

In 2011, South Dakota passed the nation's longest abortion waiting period law, three days. That means women seeking surgical abortions in that state must wait three days between their initial visit to an abortion facility and the abortion.

This is an important restriction because there are only two abortion facilities in South Dakota, and less than a quarter of South Dakota women live in counties with an abortion facility, according to the Guttmacher Institute. So for many women, obtaining an abortion means making two lengthy trips to the abortion center.

Given the legal environment in South Dakota, it's not surprising that only six percent of South Dakota women who became pregnant in 2008 aborted—three times lower than the national abortion rate of 19%. That's just 850 abortions in 2008, representing less than 0.1% of abortions nationally.

But the number of abortions performed in South Dakota likely wouldn't change much if *Roe* were overturned. In 2006, South Dakota passed a "trigger law" that would automatically ban most abortions if *Roe* is overturned. But, given that twice in the past few years South Dakota voters have voted down ballot measures to ban abortion outright, the trigger law would likely be repealed if *Roe* goes.

This means that post-*Roe* South Dakota would probably look much like it does today. Abortion would be restricted and relatively few women would obtain them. But a blanket abortion ban would be unlikely.

The same could happen in the twenty or so other states that have trigger laws or pre-*Roe* abortion bans that remain on the books. Many of these laws would be repealed or altered after *Roe*'s demise to reflect voters' opposition to total bans and legislators' unwillingness to defy public opinion.

Gerald Rosenberg, a professor at the University of Chicago who studies the effect of *Roe* on abortion rates, said recently,

"My guess is that no more than a dozen states could sustain a total abortion ban, and these are principally states where virtually no legal abortions are performed today."

Now consider California, where there are no major restrictions to abortion and only 1% of women live in counties without an abortion facility.

Abortion is available virtually on demand in California, and, in 2008, nearly one quarter of the 900,000 California women who got pregnant aborted. That's 214,109 abortions, or nearly one-fifth of all abortions nationally.

But California's high abortion rate probably wouldn't change much were *Roe* overturned. California is one of seven states that have passed laws that, according to Guttmacher, "prohibit any interference with a woman exercising her right to obtain an abortion before viability or when necessary to protect the life and health of the woman."

In other words, these seven states—which together account for one quarter of abortions nationally—have passed laws that codify *Roe.*

The Center for Reproductive Rights estimates that 23 states would protect abortion fully if *Roe* fell. According to the Guttmacher statistics, these states accounted for 713,120 abortions in 2008, or 59% of abortions nationally.

The upshot is that *Roe* means relatively little in terms of the number of abortions because the vast majority of abortions take place in states that would almost certainly keep the practice legal if *Roe* fell, and relatively few abortions take place in states that would ban the procedure.

But that doesn't mean *Roe* isn't important. I asked experts on both sides of the debate whether *Roe* still matters. Not surprisingly, they all responded emphatically that it does.

Susan Cohen, director of Government Affairs with the Guttmacher Institute, told me that because many states might "jump to criminalize abortion" if *Roe* were overturned, *Roe* "has never been more relevant or critical in maintaining basic protections and rights for American women."

Denise Burke of Americans United for Life, a pro-life legal organization that creates model pro-life legislation for states, told me that *Roe*'s reversal is important because, among other things, *Roe* is "the paradigmatic case of judicial usurpation of the legislative role." She says that striking it down would take away the federal courts' power to decide abortion policy and block laws passed by the people's elected representatives.

Robert George, McCormick Professor of Jurisprudence at Princeton University, wrote in an email that even a relatively small drop in abortions after *Roe* would be "well worth doing" because "each human life spared is of inestimable value."

But George thinks pro-lifers shouldn't be satisfied with merely working to overturn *Roe*. He believes they should also work for federal protection of unborn human life. He believes abortion is not purely a state issue and that the 14th Amendment to the Constitution expressly empowers Congress to enforce through legislation the guarantees of due process and equal protection to unborn human beings as persons.

George also mentioned the "enormous symbolic significance" of *Roe* and the corresponding symbolic significance that its reversal would have.

Michael New, an assistant professor at the University of Michigan–Dearborn who studies abortion trends, conceded that *Roe*'s reversal wouldn't significantly change the legal status of abortion in many states.

But because "the law is a powerful teacher," he thinks overturning *Roe* "would be an important first step for the pro-life movement. . . . For the first time in nearly 40 years it would result in a meaningful national debate about what sort of legal protection unborn children deserve."

Carol Tobias, president of National Right to Life, agreed. "*Roe* is still relevant," she said. Tobias referred to *Roe*'s reversal as "a teaching tool," because as long as *Roe* remains, nine un-elected justices are setting abortion policy for the entire country.

Roe's demise, in Tobias's formulation, would be "a beginning not an end." If that's true, it's a beginning pro-lifers have been waiting 39 years to commence.

Periodical and Internet Sources Bibliography

The following articles have been selected to supplement the diverse views presented in this chapter.

Aaron Blake — "Why Republicans Should Stop Talking About *Roe v. Wade*," *Washington Post*, January 22, 2013.

Irin Carmon — "5 Things You Don't Know About *Roe*," *Salon*, January 22, 2013. www.salon.com.

Ross Douthat — "Divided by Abortion, United by Feminism," *New York Times*, January 26, 2013.

The Economist — "*Roe* Turns 40: Abortion Law," January 26, 2013.

Katrina vanden Heuvel — "Chipping Away at *Roe v. Wade*," *Washington Post*, January 22, 2013.

Anna Higgins — "What the Polls Really Show About *Roe v. Wade*," *Human Events*, January 23, 2013.

National Review Online — "An Enduring Wrong," January 22, 2013. www.nationalreview.com.

New York Sun — "Is *Roe v. Wade* Moot?," January 22, 2013.

Jessica Prol — "March for Life Marks 40 Years of Abortion Law," *Washington Times*, January 25, 2013.

William Sullivan — "Deconstructing *Roe v. Wade*," *American Thinker*, January 24, 2013. www.americanthinker.com.

George Weigel — "Pro-life Rising, Forty Years after *Roe v. Wade*," *First Things*, January 23, 2013.

OPPOSING
VIEWPOINTS®
SERIES

CHAPTER 3

Should Abortion Rights Be Restricted?

Chapter Preface

Despite the fact that abortion in early pregnancy has been constitutionally protected since the US Supreme Court's decision in *Roe v. Wade* in 1973, decades later the controversy about abortion still remains. Although there has always been political debate about whether *Roe* should be overturned, in recent years the debate has come to focus more on what kind of restrictions there should be on legal abortion. Opponents of abortion have focused their strategies on the passing of state laws to restrict abortion to earlier stages of pregnancy.

In *Roe v. Wade*, the Court prohibited states from making abortion illegal prior to the stage at which the state is justified in protecting the fetus. The Court explained this point as occurring at viability:

> With respect to the State's important and legitimate interest in potential life, the "compelling" point is at viability. This is so because the fetus then presumably has the capability of meaningful life outside the mother's womb. State regulation protective of fetal life after viability thus has both logical and biological justifications. If the State is interested in protecting fetal life after viability, it may go so far as to proscribe abortion during that period, except when it is necessary to preserve the life or health of the mother.

The Court at the time noted, "Viability is usually placed at about seven months (28 weeks) but may occur earlier, even at 24 weeks." Since the third trimester starts at 28 weeks, since *Roe v. Wade* it was understood that states may not ban abortion until the third trimester.

Although *Roe v. Wade* allows states to ban abortion in the third trimester, not all states do so. In 2010, Nebraska passed a law banning abortion at 20 weeks, citing the existence of fetal pain as justification for the restriction. In the years following, several other states enacted similar bans. Because these laws are not based on fetal viability, the constitutionality of the laws under *Roe v. Wade* is in dispute. In fact, 20-week abortion bans in Arizona and Idaho have been struck down as unconstitutional. In 2013, North Dakota passed a law prohibiting abortion after 6 weeks and Arkansas passed a ban on abortion at 12 weeks, both citing presence of a fetal heartbeat as justification for the bans. The courts temporarily blocked the enactments of both abortion restrictions, while a legal battle ensues.

Whether all judges will reach the conclusion that abortion bans prior to viability are unconstitutional, or whether the issue will make its way to the US Supreme Court, remains to be seen. What is clear, however, is that the battle in the United States about abortion has shifted from a debate about whether *Roe v. Wade* should be overturned to a host of debates about the ways in which abortion can be regulated and restricted, as the the viewpoints in this chapter illustrate.

> "*[The National Right to Life Committee] strongly supports a bill that . . . would prohibit the abortion of unborn children . . . after . . . 20 weeks after fertilization.*"

Abortions Should Be Restricted to Before Twenty Weeks Gestation

Douglas Johnson

In the following viewpoint Douglas Johnson argues that the District of Columbia should join several other states in passing the Pain-Capable Unborn Child Protection Act, which would prohibit abortion for pregnancies advanced beyond twenty weeks after conception. Johnson claims new evidence proves that fetuses are capable of experiencing pain by twenty weeks, if not sooner, and that the age of fetus viability is getting lower and lower. Johnson is legislative director for the National Right to Life Committee.

As you read, consider the following questions:

1. Which five states enacted the Pain-Capable Unborn Child Protection Act during 2010 and 2011, according to the author?

2. According to Johnson, the Pain-Capable Unborn Child Protection Act prohibits abortion after twenty weeks with what exceptions?

3. Infants as early as how many weeks can commonly survive in neonatal intensive care units, according to the author?

The Supreme Court's 1973 decision in *Roe v. Wade* was issued during the "Dark Ages" in terms of pre-natal medical science. In the ensuing decades, knowledge regarding the development of unborn humans, and their capacities at various stages of growth, has advanced in quantum leaps.

For example, improvements in ultrasound and other imaging technologies have allowed doctors to see smaller and smaller details of the unborn child's anatomy. The first open-womb fetal surgery was performed in 1981, and such procedures are now routine at a number of facilities. During fetal surgery, physicians were able to observe unborn children reacting to painful stimuli, and this was one major factor that led to the current recommended practice of administering anaesthesia to the unborn child at around 20 weeks.

Implications for Abortion Policy

It is long past time for lawmakers to take note of these developments and the implications that they should have for abortion policy. . . . Five states have already done so, during 2010 and 2011, by enacting the NRLC [National Right to Life Committee]-backed Pain-Capable Unborn Child Protection Act. Those states are Nebraska, Kansas, Idaho, Oklahoma, and Alabama.

In these states, legislatures have adopted factual findings regarding the medical evidence that unborn children experience pain at least by 20 weeks after fertilization (which is about the start of the sixth month, in layperson's terminology), and they therefore prohibit abortion after that point, with narrowly drawn exceptions. There has been no serious legal challenge mounted to any of these laws.

Additional state legislatures will be considering such legislation during the months ahead, including Virginia, Florida, and New Hampshire.

Under the U.S. Constitution, the members of these state legislatures have the primary responsibility for enacting laws to protect members of the human family within their respective borders—although that responsibility is shared with the Congress. But under the Constitution, there is one substantial area in which legislative responsibility is invested *solely and directly* in the Congress, which is "such District . . . as may . . . become the seat of the government of the United States."

A District of Columbia Bill

With respect to this Federal District, Congress shall "exercise exclusive legislation in all cases whatsoever," according to the Constitution. You cannot get much plainer than that. Congress has chosen to delegate certain powers and municipal functions, but members of Congress cannot (absent a constitutional amendment) escape the fact that they alone hold ultimate responsibility for the laws that govern the Federal District.

We believe that it will come as a shock to many Americans to learn that in the federal city, the capital of our nation, abortion now is allowed for any reason at any point in pregnancy. Moreover, abortions are being performed on demand, and are openly advertised, far past the point at which an unborn child becomes pain capable.

The Pain-Capable Unborn Child Protection Act

The states that have passed the Pain-Capable Unborn Child Protection Act as of April 30, 2013:

TAKEN FROM: National Right to Life Committee, "States That Protect Pain-Capable Unborn Children," April 30, 2013. www.nrlc.org

Therefore, NRLC strongly supports a bill that will be introduced today, in the U.S. House of Representatives, by Congressman Trent Franks, Republican of Arizona, which would prohibit the abortion of unborn children in the Federal District after the point that the Congress finds substantial evidence exists that they experience pain, which this bill—like the bills enacted by five states—defines as 20 weeks after fertilization, which is 22 weeks in the "last menstrual period" system of calculation, or about the beginning of the sixth month in layperson's terminology. The bill contains carefully drawn exceptions for circumstances in which a pregnant woman suffers from an acute, life-endangering physical condition.

Again, on this matter—a matter of life and death, painful death—the buck stops entirely with Congress. If at the end of this congressional session, abortion remains unrestricted in the nation's capital, during the sixth, seventh, eighth, and ninth months, it will be because certain members of Congress, or the President, have obstructed this bill. If they do that, then they alone, under the Constitution, are fully accountable for that policy.

Evidence of Fetal Pain

We believe that there is abundant evidence to support the findings contained in Congressman Frank's bill. Indeed, if it were not for what we might call the "abortion distortion" factor, there would not even be an argument about this. The evidence that unborn members of the species homo sapiens, by the beginning of the sixth month (if not well earlier), are capable of experiencing excruciating pain would be accepted without serious dispute, if it did not bear on the question of the availability of induced abortion.

Consider the words of the preeminent pioneer researcher in the pain-perception capacities of premature infants, Dr. Kanwaljeet S. Anand, who said in a document accepted as expert by a federal court, "It is my opinion that the human fetus possesses the ability to experience pain from 20 weeks of gestation, if not earlier, and that pain perceived by a fetus is possibly more intense than that perceived by newborns or older children."

Infants born as early as 23 or 24 weeks now commonly survive long term in neonatal intensive care units. Neonataologists confirm that they react negatively to painful stimuli—for example, by grimacing, withdrawing, and whimpering. When they must receive surgical procedures, they are given drugs to prevent pain.

Yet, some pro-abortion advocates want you to believe an unborn baby who is at exactly the same stage of development experiences no discomfort as her arms and legs are literally twisted off, by brute manual force, in the common procedure known as dilation and evacuation (or "D&E"), or stabbed through the heart with a needle. Some of the supposed medical authorities quoted in the press as asserting that human fetuses cannot feel pain until 29 weeks or later have themselves performed thousands of late abortions—and all too often, that fact is not disclosed in the stories quoting these supposed voices of scientific authority.

In any event, the members of Congress will have the opportunity to evaluate these competing claims, and to determine whether the weight of evidence is sufficient to justify the findings in this legislation, and the public policy which it proposes to adopt for the Federal city on that basis.

> *"The consequences of [restricting abortion to before twenty weeks] will be inhumane."*

Restricting Abortion to Before Twenty Weeks Gestation Would Be Inhumane

Christy Zink

In the following viewpoint Christy Zink argues that the attempt to pass legislation banning abortion after twenty weeks is misguided. Zink claims that such legislation is influenced by a misunderstanding about the kind of women who seek late-term abortions, providing an account of her own late-term abortion as an example of how such a decision comes about to many women. Zink contends that late-term abortion is a tragedy for most women and urges Congress to leave the decision to abort up to women and their doctors. Zink is director of the University Writing Center at the George Washington University in Washington, DC.

As you read, consider the following questions:

1. The author claims that she had an abortion at twenty-two weeks of pregnancy for what reason?

2. The author cites a study finding that abortions after twenty-one weeks make up what percentage of all abortions in the United States?

3. What effects does Zink claim that passage of the proposed bill would have on real women and families?

Introduce me to the woman who has an abortion after 20 weeks because she is cruel and heartless. Introduce me to the lazy gal who gets knocked up and ignores her condition until, more than halfway through her pregnancy, she ends it because it has become too darn inconvenient for her selfish lifestyle.

The Myth About Late Abortion

If such a woman exists, I have never met her. Sadly, however, she appears to have influenced the thinking of even savvy, politically informed people in this country. Otherwise, how could they argue that carrying to term is always the right decision late in pregnancy? In fact, the myth of such callous women has been compelling enough to push along a bill that would ban abortion in the District after 20 weeks of pregnancy; the bill was approved this month [July 2012] by the House Judiciary Committee, moving it forward for consideration by the full House, perhaps as soon as Tuesday [July 31].

Believing this fabrication of the radical right depends on one's ability to conjure at once a perfectly unfeeling woman and a perfectly healthy child, a stand-in for the much more tragic and complex reality. Meet, instead, a real live, breathing woman who terminated a much-wanted pregnancy at almost 22 weeks, when her baby was found to have severe fetal anomalies of the brain.

My son's condition could not have been detected earlier in the pregnancy. Far from lazy, I was conscientious about prenatal care. I received excellent medical attention from my obstetrician, one of the District's best. Only at our 20-week sonogram were there warning signs, and only with a high-powered MRI [magnetic resonance imaging scan] did we discover the devastating truth of our son's condition. He was missing the corpus callosum, the central connecting structure of the brain, and essentially one side of his brain.

If he survived the pregnancy and birth, the doctors told us, he would have been born into a life of continuous seizures and near-constant pain. He might never have left the hospital. To help control the seizures, he would have needed surgery to remove more of what little brain matter he had. That was the reality for me and for my family.

Women Who Have Late Abortions

Meet, too, the many real women I know who belong to one of the saddest groups in the world: those carrying babies for whom there was no real hope and who made the heartbreaking decision to end their pregnancies for medical reasons. Meet the women among this group who had gotten, they thought, safely to the middle of pregnancy, who had been planning nurseries and filling baby registries, only to find they would need to plan a memorial service and to build, somehow, a life in the aftermath.

We are not reckless, ruthless creatures. Our hearts hurt each day for our losses. We mourn. We speak the names and nicknames of each other's babies to one another; we hold each other up on the anniversaries of our losses, and we celebrate new babies and new accomplishments, all bittersweet because they arrive in the wake of grief. We extend our arms to the women who must join our community, and we lament that our numbers rise every day.

Medical research from the Guttmacher Institute shows that post-21-week terminations make up less than 2 percent of all abortions in this country. Women like me can seem an exception. You also rarely hear stories like mine, because they involve intensely private sorrow and because there is no small

When Women Have Abortions

Eighty-eight percent of abortions in 2006 occured in the first twelve weeks of pregancy.

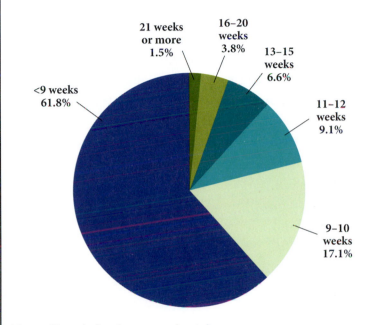

21 weeks
or more
1.5%

16–20
weeks
3.8%

13–15
weeks
6.6%

<9 weeks
61.8%

11–12
weeks
9.1%

9–10
weeks
17.1%

Measured in weeks from last menstrual period.

TAKEN FROM: Guttmacher Institute, "Facts on Induced Abortion in the United States," October 2013. www.guttmacher.org.

amount of shame still associated with terminating a pregnancy, no matter how medically necessary.

An Inhumane Law

The consequences of the House bill, if it becomes law, will be inhumane. If the restrictions in this bill had been the law of the land when my husband and I received our diagnosis, I would have had to carry to term and give birth to a baby who the doctors concurred had no chance of a real life and who would have faced severe, continual pain. The decision my husband and I made to terminate the pregnancy was made out of love—to spare my son pain and suffering.

The ugly politics in this Congress and the sheer number of Republicans mean that this bill will likely pass in the House [the bill passed the House but not the Senate]. I understand any citizen's hesitancy when the issue of the right to middle-term to late-term abortion arises. But I also know from my own experience that this bill would have calamitous ramifications for real women and real families, and that the women it would most affect could never imagine they would need their right to abortion protected in this way.

Women and their families must be able to trust their doctors and retain their access to medical care when they most need it. To make sure that happens, members of the Senate and ordinary people across this country must see through the stereotype of the late-term aborter and see, instead, the true face of a woman who has been in this situation. I extend my hand; it is an honor to make your acquaintance.

> *"Parental consent laws boast a 71 percent nationwide approval rating, protect the health and well-being of minors, respect parental rights, and save the lives of unborn babies."*

Parental-Involvement Laws for Abortion Protect Minors and Parents

Mary E. Harned

In the following viewpoint Mary E. Harned argues that parental involvement laws regarding abortion—including parental-notification laws and parental-consent laws—protect minors and parents. Harned contends that current parental-notification laws could benefit from better enforcement and more stringent requirements. She argues that clarification is needed for courts in assessing a minor's maturity level, should a minor use the courts to attempt to bypass the parental-involvement requirement. Harned is staff counsel for Americans United for Life, a nonprofit pro-life law and policy organization.

Mary E. Harned, "Parental Involvement Laws: Protecting Minors and Parental Rights," *Defending Life in 2013: Deconstruction Roe v. Wade.* (DC: Americans United for Life, 2013). Copyright © 2013 by Americans United for Life. All rights reserved. Reproduced by permission.

As you read, consider the following questions:

1. According to the author, a 2008 study found that parental-consent laws reduce the minor abortion rate by what percent?

2. What is one of the potential loopholes, according to the author, in current parental-involvement laws?

3. Harned suggests using what standard of proof for assessing the truth of the factual matter at issue in a judicial bypass proceeding?

In 2011, Connecticut—one of only 12 states without a law requiring parental consent or notification before a minor may obtain an abortion—drew national attention when legislative consideration of a bill that would require parental consent for the use of tanning parlors evolved into an abortion debate. One brave legislator confronted his colleagues with a disturbing fact: while the state requires parental consent for tattooing and body piercing, and intended to extend that requirement to the use of tanning parlors, minors may obtain an abortion in Connecticut without any parental involvement. However, when the state senator tried to add a provision requiring parental consent for abortion to the bill, the legislature abandoned it altogether.

Support for Parental Involvement Laws

It is difficult to comprehend the Connecticut legislature's strong opposition to a law requiring parental consent prior to a minor's abortion, when parental consent laws boast a 71 percent nationwide approval rating, protect the health and well-being of minors, respect parental rights, and save the lives of unborn babies. In fact, this popular legislation saw a rebirth in 2011, with at least 24 states considering one or more measures to enact new or strengthen existing consent or notification requirements.

Why the interest in and support for these laws? The medical, emotional, and psychological consequences of abortion are often serious and can be lasting, particularly when the patient is immature. Moreover, parents usually possess information essential to a physician's exercise of his or her best medical judgment concerning the minor. Parents who are aware that their daughter has had an abortion may better ensure the best post-abortion medical attention. Further, minors who obtain "secret" abortions often do so at the behest of the older men who impregnated them, and then return to abusive situations. News stories frequently reveal yet another teen that has been sexually abused by a person in authority—a coach, teacher, or other authority figure. Every day, teens are taken to abortion clinics without the consent or even the knowledge of their parents. Minors are at risk in every state in which parental involvement laws have not been enacted or are easily circumvented.

In addition, parental involvement laws save the lives of unborn babies by reducing the demand for abortions by minors. For example, a 1996 study revealed that "parental involvement laws appear to decrease minors' demands for abortion by 13 to 25 percent." A 2008 study showed that parental consent laws reduce the minor abortion rate by 18.7 percent. With the loving support of their parents, many young women are able to bring their babies into the world and not face the physical risks and emotional devastation that abortions can bring.

The Supreme Court's Guidelines

The U.S. Supreme Court has reviewed statutes requiring parental consent or notification before a minor may obtain an abortion on 11 different occasions. The Court's decisions in these cases provide state legislators with concrete guidelines on how to draft parental involvement laws that will be upheld by the courts.

Based upon Supreme Court precedent and subsequent lower federal court decisions, a parental involvement law is constitutional and does not place an undue burden on minors if it contains the following provisions:

For consent, no physician may perform an abortion upon a minor or incompetent person unless the physician has the consent of one parent or legal guardian. For notice, no physician may perform an abortion upon a minor or incompetent person unless the physician performing the abortion has given 48 hours notice to a parent or legal guardian of the minor or incompetent person.

An exception to the consent or notice requirement exists when there is a medical emergency or when notice is waived by the person entitled to receive the notice.

A minor may bypass the requirement through the courts (i.e., judicial waiver or bypass).

AUL [Americans United for Life] has drafted both a model "Parental Consent for Abortion Act" as well as a "Parental Notification of Abortion Act," which are based upon Supreme Court precedent and take these issues into consideration.

The Judicial Bypass Requirement

In *Bellotti v. Baird (Bellotti II)* [1979], the Court held that a state which requires a pregnant minor to obtain one or both parents' consent to an abortion must "provide an alternative procedure whereby authorization for the abortion can be obtained." This procedure must include the following four elements:

- An allowance for the minor to show that "she is mature enough and well enough informed to make her abortion decision, in consultation with her physician, independently of her parents' wishes;"

- An allowance for the minor to alternatively show that "even if she is not able to make this decision independently, the desired abortion would be in her best interests;"

- The proceedings in which one of these showings is made must be "completed with anonymity;" and

- The proceedings in which one of these showings is made must be "completed with . . . sufficient expedition to provide an effective opportunity for an abortion to be obtained."

In *Ohio v. Akron Center for Reproductive Health (Akron II)* [1990], the Court left open the question of whether a statute requiring parental notice rather than consent required bypass procedures. The Court stated that given "the greater intrusiveness of consent statutes . . . a bypass procedure that will suffice for a consent statute will suffice also for a notice statute." In other words, when a state includes in its parental notification law bypass procedures that meet the constitutional requirements for a consent bypass, the state's bypass procedures are unquestionably constitutional.

In the 1992 case *Planned Parenthood v. Casey*, a plurality of the United States Supreme Court reaffirmed that a state may constitutionally "require a minor seeking an abortion to obtain the consent of a parent or guardian, provided that there is an adequate judicial bypass procedure." The Court further held that an exception to the parental consent requirement for a "medical emergency" was sufficient to protect a minor's health, and imposed "no undue burden" on her access to abortion.

The Supreme Court noted that the Court of Appeals construed the phrase "serious risk" in the definition of "medical emergency" to include serious conditions that would affect the health of the minor. The lower court stated, "We read the medical emergency exception as intended by the Pennsylvania

American Opinion on Parental Consent

When it comes to specific restrictions, Americans overwhelmingly support requiring women under age 18 to get the consent of at least one parent before having an abortion (76%), a figure that is largely unchanged in recent years. Large majorities of conservative Republicans (89%), white evangelicals (83%) and opponents of legal abortion (83%) express support for parental consent laws. But support for parental consent legislation is high even among those groups whose members are more supportive of abortion rights. For example, large majorities of the religiously unaffiliated (64%), mainline Protestants (77%) and Catholics (81%) favor requiring parental consent. Even among those who say abortion should be legal in most or all cases, 71% favor requiring parental consent.

Pew Forum on Religion and Public Life,
October 1, 2009. www.pewforum.org.

legislature to assure that compliance with its abortion regulations would not in any way pose a significant threat to the life or health of a woman." Based on this reading, the Court in *Casey* held that the medical emergency definition "imposes no undue burden on a woman's abortion right."

The Need for Enhancements

Tragically, it is often easy for abortion providers to sidestep a law requiring parental consent or notice by claiming they were "duped" into accepting consent from or providing notice to individuals fraudulently representing themselves as the parents or guardians of minors. Other potential loopholes in parental consent or notice statutes include: the inappropriate use of an emergency exception by an abortion provider; exploitation of the judicial bypass system through "forum shopping" (finding courts likely to grant a judicial bypass); a low burden of proof for a minor to show that she is mature enough to make her own abortion decision, or that parental consent or notice is not in her best interest; and a lack of guidance to courts on how to evaluate a minor's maturity or what is in her best interest.

To assist states in better protecting minors and parental rights, AUL has drafted the "Parental Involvement Enhancement Act" to reinforce existing parental involvement laws with the enhancements discussed below.

In parental consent states, a consenting parent or guardian should be required to present government-issued identification before a minor obtains an abortion. In parental notice states, a parent or guardian should be required to present identification when waiving the right to notice. In addition to providing identification, a parent or guardian should provide documentation proving that they are the parent or legal guardian of the minor seeking an abortion. Copies of the identification and proof of relationship must then be kept by the abortion clinic in the minor's medical records. When such actions are required, ignorance of an adult's true identity is not an excuse for failing to follow the law.

Another method states may utilize to ensure that the appropriate person is providing consent or waiving notice is to require the notarization of the applicable form(s). Like the identification and proof of relationship requirements discussed above, notarization requirements help ensure that the correct person has consented or has been notified of plans to perform an abortion on a minor. Further, it is difficult for abortion providers to subvert this requirement.

A "medical emergency" exception in parental involvement laws should not be a license for abortion providers to circumvent the law. Further, a minor who has an abortion following a medical emergency will often require more follow-up care and support from her parents or guardians. Therefore, states can ensure that parental involvement laws are not circumvented and that minors are better protected by requiring abortion providers to promptly notify a parent or guardian that a minor had an "emergency" abortion, the reason for the abortion, and a description of necessary follow-up care.

Preventing Easy Waivers

Some judges or courts are more inclined to grant judicial waiver requests than others. Undoubtedly, abortion providers know which judges or courts are "friendly" to subverting parental rights, and may guide minors to seek a bypass in those courts. To prevent this and better protect minors, states may require a minor to seek a bypass in a court of jurisdiction within her home county.

States may require courts to find "clear and convincing evidence"—evidence showing a high probability of truth of the factual matter at issue—that a minor is either: 1) sufficiently mature and well-informed to consent to an abortion without parental involvement; or 2) that an abortion without parental involvement is in her best interest. "Clear and convincing evidence" is an intermediate standard of proof—higher than "preponderance of the evidence" (more likely than not), but lower than "beyond a reasonable doubt" (used in criminal cases). While judges have broad discretion under most parental involvement laws (their decision to grant a bypass is not subject to review), the "clear and convincing evidence" standard better ensures that judges carefully examine and weigh the facts presented to them in bypass proceedings.

Courts benefit from the provision of specific standards for judicial review in evaluating judicial bypass petitions. Currently, most consent and notice requirements contain very basic criteria, simply requiring that the minor be mature enough to make the decision, or requiring that the abortion be in the minor's "best interest."

Criteria for Assessing Maturity

An Arizona appellate court case delineated criteria that a judge should use in evaluating the maturity of a minor petitioning for judicial bypass. Specifically, the court's decision:

- Endorsed an examination of the minor's "experience, perspective, and judgment"; Defined "experience" as "all that has happened to the minor in her lifetime including things she has seen or done;"

- Provided that, in assessing a minor's experience level, the court should consider such things as the minor's age and experiences working outside the home, living away from home, handling personal finances, and making other "significant decisions;"

- Defined "perspective," in the context of an abortion decision as the "minor's ability to appreciate and understand the relative gravity and possible detrimental impact of available options, as well as the potential consequences of each;"

- Recommended that, in assessing a minor's perspective on her abortion decision, the court should examine the steps she took to explore her options and the extent to which she considered and weighed the potential consequences of each option;

- Defined "judgment" as the "minor's intellectual and emotional ability to make the abortion decision without the [involvement] of her parents or guardians;"

- Provided that, in assessing judgment, the court should examine the minor's conduct since learning of her pregnancy and her intellectual ability to understand her options and make an informed decision.

This decision provides an excellent example of how, based upon Supreme Court precedent, the more basic judicial bypass requirements can be enhanced.

To further assist courts with their evaluation, states may permit a court to refer a minor for a mental health evaluation. This type of measure protects minors from their own immaturity or from coercion or abuse by others.

| "*Laws that mandate parental involvement in teens' abortions offer anti-choice judges new opportunities to limit abortion access.*"

Parental Involvement Laws Threaten the Safety of Minors

Nina Liss-Schultz

In the following viewpoint Nina Liss-Schultz argues that state laws that require parental notice or parental consent or leave it up to the Court's decision prior to allowing a minor to get an abortion endanger the health and well being of young women. Laws that require parental consent offer anti-choice judges new opportunities to limit abortion access. They also limit teens' freedom to make their own choices and potentially put teens at risk. Shultz is an online editor for Mother Jones.

As you read, consider the following questions:

1. According to the author, what are some of the risks of parental consent or parental notification laws?

2. How many states require some kind of parental involvement in a minor's decision to have an abortion, according to the author?

3. According to Shultz, what does a "judicial bypass" have the power to do in relation to parental involement laws?

The Nebraska Supreme Court ruled on Friday that a 16-year-old could not get the abortion she wanted because she "was not mature enough to make the decision herself." The Court's ability to force the teen, a ward of the state known only as Anonymous 5, to carry her unwanted child to term is a direct result of the state's 2011 parental consent law that requires minors seeking an abortion to get parental approval.

Parental Involvement Laws Limit Abortion Access

But Nebraska is not unique: similar rulings could happen in most other states across the country. Laws that mandate parental involvement in teens' abortions offer anti-choice judges new opportunities to limit abortion access. And while it is unclear whether such parental involvement legislation affects minors' abortion rates in general, Sharon Camp, former president and CEO of Guttmacher Institute, wrote in an article for RH Reality Check that such mandates can put teens at risk of physical violence or abuse and "result in teens' delaying abortions until later in pregnancy, when they carry a greater risk of complications and are also more expensive to obtain." The case of the Nebraska teen also shows that parental involvement legislation overlooks wards of the state, leaving pregnant young adults who have no legal parents at the behest of the court system.

According to Guttmacher, "only two states and the District of Columbia explicitly allow" all minors to consent to their own abortions. On the other hand, a whopping 39 states require some kind of parental involvement in a minor's decision to have an abortion.

There are two major types of legislation mandating parental involvement in their child's decision to have an abortion:

Parental consent and parental notification laws. Parental consent laws mandate that a minor who has decided to get an abortion first get the OK from either one or both of her parents (or her legal guardian). Parental notification laws, on the other hand, require that a parent or legal guardian be notified of a child's decision to get an abortion, either by the minor herself or by her doctor. Eight states, including Nebraska, mandate a notarized statement of consent from a parent before the abortion is performed. And in Arkansas, the Governor recently signed a law making it a crime to assist a minor in obtaining an abortion without her parent's consent, "even if the abortion was performed in a state where parental consent is not required."

Parental Involvement Law Exceptions

Almost all states with parental involvement laws include some exceptions to the rules. Many states allow exceptions in medical emergencies or in cases of abuse, assault, incest, or neglect. Only a handful of states extend their consent or notification laws to other adult relatives, like grandparents.

But one exception in particular has increased the role of the courts in the personal decision-making of teens. As a result of a Supreme Court ruling that parents cannot have complete veto power in determining whether their child gets an abortion, almost all states offer a "judicial bypass" to their parental involvement laws. The bypass allows minors to go to the courts to waive their state's involvement laws; but in effect moves the power to veto a teen's abortion from her family to the courts.

And here is where the Nebraska case comes in. In this case, the biological parents of Anonymous 5 had previously been stripped of their legal parental rights after physically abusing their daughter and, as a result, the pregnant teen had no legal parents and was instead a ward of the state. With no parent to consent to her abortion, she was forced to ask permission from the courts, who then denied her request, essentially finding her mature enough to carry a baby she doesn't want but too immature to consent to her own abortion. Instead of offering an alternative to parental consent, the courts serve as just another barrier between teens—especially wards of the state—and access to safe abortion services.

Periodical and Internet Sources Bibliography

The following articles have been selected to supplement the diverse views presented in this chapter.

Colleen Carroll Campbell	"A Reality Check Before an Abortion," *St. Louis Post Dispatch*, May 6, 2010.
Michelle Chen	"It's Not Just Forced Ultrasound: Abortion Rights Under Assault," *Salon*, October 21, 2012. www.salon.com.
David Christensen	"Abortion and the Live-and-Let-Live Ethic," *Daily Caller*, January 18, 2013. http://dailycaller.com.
Marjorie Dannenfelser	"Planned Parenthood Cranks Up Abortion Mills: Federal Subsidies Grow to Record Levels," *Washington Times*, January 22, 2013.
Paula Gianino	"40 Years Safe and Legal: Let's Keep It That Way," *St. Louis Post-Dispatch*, January 22, 2013.
Joey Hendrix	"Abortions for Soldiers at US Military Bases?," *Christian Science Monitor*, July 21, 2010.
Marian V. Liautaud	"Shouldn't a Ban on Sex-Selective Abortions in America Be a No-Brainer?," Her-meneutics, June 8, 2012. www.christianitytoday.com.
Michael Stokes Paulsen	"War on Women," *Weekly Standard*, January 22, 2013.
Jeffrey Toobin	"The People's Choice," *New Yorker*, January 28, 2013.
Rick Ungar	"Virginia's Pre-Abortion Ultrasound Law Medically Unsound—Violates Guidelines of American College Of Obstetricians and Gynecologists," *Forbes*, March 8, 2012.

CHAPTER 4

What Are Some Medical and Social Concerns About Abortion?

Chapter Preface

Beyond the debate about the morality of abortion are other concerns about abortion related to how it impacts the health of women who choose abortion and how abortion impacts the rest of society. Since the US Supreme Court's 1973 *Roe v. Wade* decision, women have been able to choose to terminate pregnancy in the early stages for any reason they see fit. As prenatal testing advances, allowing women to gain more information about the fetus earlier in a pregnancy, there is growing concern that women will choose abortion more frequently to try to avoid having a baby with certain traits. There is controversy about using abortion to eliminate offspring with certain diseases, but perhaps even more controversial is the concern that abortion is being used to eliminate fetuses of an unwanted gender, most often those that are female.

According to researchers, the sex ratio at birth is fairly consistent across populations, with approximately 106 males born for every 100 females, a 1.06 ratio. According to the Central Intelligence Agency's (CIA's) 2013 *World Factbook*, several countries around the world had male-to-female birth ratios that seem to demand an explanation beyond chance: Albania and Georgia (in the Caucasus region of Eurasia) had a rate of 1.10; Armenia had a sex ratio at birth of 1.11; and China, India, and Vietnam had rates of 1.12. The Guttmacher Institute claims that some provinces in China and some regions in India have a sex ratio of 1.30. It is believed that such skewed sex ratios are signs of sex-selective abortion or infanticide.

Mara Hvistendahl, author of *Unnatural Selection: Choosing Boys over Girls and the Consequences of a World Full of Men*, claims that sex-selective abortion resulted in 163 million fewer girls who would have been born over the past decades in Asia. The cultural value of having boys over girls in certain parts of

Asia has resulted in a preference for boys that is believed to be sometimes achieved through sex-selective abortion. In addition, there is reason to believe that sex-selective abortion also occurs in the United States. Several studies of Chinese, Korean, and East Indian immigrant parents in the United States found skewed sex ratios for later children, with fewer girls, suggesting evidence of sex-selective abortion.

Concern about sex-selective abortion prompted the Susan B. Anthony and Frederick Douglass Prenatal Nondiscrimination Act of 2011 and the Prenatal Nondiscrimination Act (PRENDA) of 2012, neither of which passed. These bills would outlaw abortion based on sex selection or race selection. A similar bill, the Prenatal Nondiscrimination Act (PRENDA) of 2013, was introduced and referred to committee in 2013 and, as of this writing, is still under consideration. Thus, the concern about sex-selective abortion is ongoing.

The viewpoints in the following chapter debate some of the issues regarding some of the medical and social concerns surrounding abortion.

▌ *"Abortion can be deadly for women."*

Studies Show Abortion May Increase Premature Death, Breast Cancer Risk

Dave Bohon

In the following viewpoint Dave Bohon argues that recent studies support the view that having an abortion is correlated with increased mortality and disease. According to Bohon, recent studies have found links between abortion and higher mortality, abortion and breast cancer, and childlessness and higher mortality. Bohon claims that mainstream researchers deny any link between breast cancer and abortion; nonetheless, Bohon claims that researchers have noted a correlation between lower mortality rates and childbearing, although they are not prepared to state that the link is causal. Bohon writes for the New American, *a publication of the conservative John Birch Society.*

As you read, consider the following questions:

1. According to the author a recent Danish study found that women who had undergone a single abortion had a higher mortality rate than childbearing women by what percentage?

2. The author claims that a study from Armenia shows that giving birth reduces the risk of breast cancer by what percentage?

3. According to Bohon, during a Danish study on child-lessness, women who gave birth were how many times more likely to be alive at the end of the study than childless women?

A recent study out of Denmark appears to show a higher incidence of premature death among women who have had an abortion than for women who give birth. The study tracked a group of Danish women over a 25-year period, finding that those who had undergone a single abortion had a 45-percent higher mortality rate over that time period than those who had carried babies to full term. The death rate among women rose dramatically for subsequent abortions, with women who had two abortions having a 114-percent greater likelihood of mortality during the study period, and women with three or more abortions facing a 192-percent chance of premature death.

David Reardon, a co-author of the study, said in a statement that the increased mortality rate among women who had subsequent abortions appears to confirm a causal relationship between the procedure and death among women. "We knew from our previous studies of low-income women in California," he explained, "that women who have multiple pregnancy outcomes, such as having a history of both abortion and miscarriage, have significantly different mortality rates."

The *Christian Post*, which reported on the study, noted that the Danish research also showed "an increase in the death rates of women who had experienced miscarriages, ectopic pregnancies or other natural losses. Women who did not have a history of loss during pregnancy were the least likely to die

The Coverup of Abortion's Risks

Abortionists in this country are actively burying risk research just as tobacco companies did many decades ago. . . .

Just as tobacco companies once deep-sixed any negative research on the smoker's health and well-being, abortionists and their extensive lobbying web of far-left, social-engineering "feminists" now scamper to squelch every new research study which demonstrates elevated risk associated with their killing-field business model. In this diabolical scheme, abortionists are far, far worse than tobacco companies could ever have been, if only for the single reason that abortion is controlled not by known capitalistic corporations, but by the very people whom the public trusts for its healthcare.

Kyle-Anne Shiver, American Thinker,
January 13, 2013. www.americanthinker.com.

during the 25 years that were examined, while women who had never conceived had the highest mortality rate."

This is not the first study showing that abortion can be deadly for women. In November 2011 LifeNews.com reported on a study showing that women who have had a single abortion may face a nearly three-fold increase in risk of breast cancer. The study, led by Dr. Lilit Khachatryan of the American University of Armenia, and which included researchers from Johns Hopkins School of Public Health and the University of Pennsylvania, also found that delaying a first full-term pregnancy significantly raised the risk of breast cancer in women, while giving birth resulted in an over 60-percent reduced risk.

"Khachatryan's team reported a statistically significant 13 percent increased breast cancer risk for every one year delay of a first full term pregnancy (FFTP)," reported LifeNews, "with delayed FFTPs until ages 21–30 or after age 30 resulting in 2.21-fold and 4.95-fold increased risks respectively." Karen Malec of the Coalition on Abortion/Breast Cancer told Life-News that the findings were not a surprise, because "54 of 67 epidemiological studies since 1957 report an abortion–breast cancer link. . . ."

In June 2010 the UK's [United Kingdom's] *Daily Mail* reported on a study from the University of Colombo in Sri Lanka that also showed a three-fold increase in risk of breast cancer among abortive women. The researchers discovered the apparent link between abortion and breast cancer "while carrying out research into how breastfeeding can protect women from developing the killer disease," reported the *Daily Mail*. "While concluding that breastfeeding offered significant protection from cancer, they also noted that the highest reported risk factor in developing the disease was abortion."

The British paper noted that the Sri Lankan research represented the "fourth epidemiological study to report such a link in the past 14 months, with research in China, Turkey, and the U.S. showing similar conclusions."

Predictably, mainstream cancer researchers cast doubt on the study, claiming that their own research has found no link between abortion and breast cancer. But Professor Jack Scarisbrick, an eminent British historian and founder of the the pro-life UK crisis pregnancy organization LIFE, insisted that the Sri Lankan study added to the "devastating" proof of the deadly link. "This study is further evidence that has been gathering from all around the world that abortion is a major risk factor for breast cancer," he said. "When will the [medical] establishment face up to this fact and pull its head out of the sand? It is betraying women by failing to warn that what they are doing to their bodies—the quick fix of abortion—can do grave harm."

Meanwhile, a recent study of a different sort offered evidence that having children is a life-saver for both men and women. The study out of Denmark tracked 21,276 Danish couples who tried to have children via *in vitro* fertilization treatments between 1994 and 2005. During the study period 15,210 children were born to the couples, 1,564 were adopted, and a total of 96 women and 200 men died over the time period.

From the data, the researchers calculated that women who gave birth were four times more likely to be alive at the end of the study period compared with women who remained childless. While the benefit to men appeared to be less significant, those who fathered children still had a two-times greater likelihood of being alive at the end of the study period than those who had not.

Similarly, those parents who could not get pregnant, but went on to adopt children, appeared to be healthier: Adoptive mothers were 33 percent less likely to die, and fathers 45 percent less likely to die, compared to their counterparts who had no children. The researchers found that the childless individuals were more likely to die from circulatory disease, cancers, and accidents than those who had children.

Lead researcher Esben Agerbo of Aarhus University in Aarhus, Denmark, told WebMD that he could only guess as to why parents with children tend to live longer. "My best guess is health behaviors," he said. "When people have kids, they tend to live healthier."

Regardless of the reason, the researchers concluded: "Mindful that association is not causation, our results suggest that the mortality rates are higher in the childless."

"Elective abortions are not associated with an increased risk of breast cancer."

The Evidence Does Not Support a Causal Link Between Abortion and Breast Cancer

Elaine Schattner

In the following viewpoint Elaine Schattner argues that recent proposed or enacted state legislation defies the principle of informed consent by promoting misinformation about the risks of abortion. Schattner contends that although research has thoroughly debunked the supposed link between abortion and breast cancer, both proponents and opponents of abortion continue to promulgate the myth. Schattner claims that too little is known about the causes of breast cancer to say what variables are causal. Schattner is a physician, medical writer, and clinical associate professor of medicine at Weill Cornell Medical College in New York City.

As you read, consider the following questions:

1. Why does Schattner say that, although disproven, the link between abortion and breast cancer was a plausible hypothesis?

2. In what year and for what reason does the author claim that the notion of a link between abortion and breast cancer gained traction?

3. The author claims that a Danish study settled the question about a link between abortion and breast cancer in what year?

In Kansas, legislators recently passed the No Taxpayer Funding for Abortion Act. If enacted into law, the bill would require doctors to tell pregnant women of a relationship between abortion and breast cancer. This news follows passage by the New Hampshire State House of the Women's Right To Know Act Regarding Abortion Information. These related laws are unlikely to gain approval by the state senates [neither passed the senate]. But there's a trend: A similar measure took effect in Texas in February [2012]. Now, providers there must inform pregnant women about "the possibility of increased risk of breast cancer following an induced abortion," the so-called ABC link.

The Cause of Breast Cancer

In the decade following *Roe v. Wade* [1973], the occurrence of breast tumors in the United States soared. The coincidental rise in case numbers with legalized abortions led some to speculate that terminating a pregnancy might boost a woman's odds. The link is plausible because female hormones and fertility influence mammary growth and tumors. After a spate of conflicting reports in the 1980s and '90s, a consensus emerged that there's no meaningful tie. Rather, modern demographics—like birth control use, delayed childbirth, and obesity—

combined with increased detection by mammography, over-whelmingly account for the rise in breast cancer diagnoses. The most recent edition of *Principles and Practice of Oncology*, the "bible" of cancer medicine, does not list abortion as a risk factor. Still, anti-abortion groups press the association.

What's curious from a med-ethics standpoint is the way in which anti-abortion activists have adopted the language of patient empowerment, like a Woman's Right To Know, and turned it upside down. The nascent laws insist that those contemplating the procedure be made aware of a falsehood or, at best, an unproved and frightening correlation. They stipulate confusion rather than informed consent.

Few doubt that a woman's reproductive history influences her chances of getting breast cancer. As early as 1703, Italian physician Bernardino Ramazzini reported that nuns suffered breast tumors with relative frequency. A century ago, the British Ministry of Health commissioned Dr. Janet Clay-Laypon to examine possible roots of the malignancy. In then-innovative case-control studies, Clay-Laypon surveyed 508 breast cancer patients at English and Scottish hospitals. For controls, she questioned women with other medical conditions. Her 1926 monograph, *A Further Report on Cancer of the Breast*, confirmed what doctors had long suspected: Women who deliver few children and marry late are more likely to develop the disease.

Today, what's known about breast cancer causes remains slim. Only a small fraction of cases trace to genetics. Having your first period at an early age or going through menopause late correlates with increased risk. Bearing multiple kids and breast-feeding may lower your risk. Hormonal birth control and replacement "therapy" after menopause are implicated too, as is radiation exposure—whether from bombs, treatment of another cancer, or too many CT [computed tomography] scans. Environmental toxins, broadly, and a few specific chemicals are named culprits, though few are incontrovertible. Other factors, (like not exercising, drinking alcohol, or being fat for older women) might increase one's chances. But essentially all the science is correlative. Absolute proof is absent.

The Abortion/Breast Cancer Link

The notion of an abortion/breast cancer link gained traction around 1981. A group of Southern California investigators observed an apparent 2.4-fold increase in breast cancer among young women who said they'd had either a miscarriage or an elective abortion in the first trimester of pregnancy. Their *British Journal of Cancer* report was limited and unusual: It included just 163 patients, all with cancer diagnoses by age 32. And the researchers' methodology was telling. They asked the women if they'd used oral contraceptives, and how many times they'd been pregnant, delivered, miscarried, or had abortions. For "controls" the investigators approached the patients' old high school friends and neighbors—literally, by going house to house on the blocks where they lived—and posed to them the same personal questions.

Between 1980 and 1997, scientists produced dozens of reports on the putative ABC link, finding one side or the other in rough tandem with political outbursts over abortion rights. Clinicians, evidently, were oblivious: In a study of California physicians' attitudes about breast cancer, none mentioned abortion among 29 possible causes.

The overriding problem is that abortion's a loaded subject. Same goes for breast cancer. Recall bias weighs heavily in case-control studies on topics like these, limiting or abrogating their value. It's not unusual for breast cancer patients to feel ashamed of their illness. Some pore over the details of their moral and physical past selves, wondering what they've done to cause the ailment. Even if they don't feel guilty, patients may think that knowing they've had an abortion could make a difference in doctors' understanding of their medical condi-

Abortion and Risk of Cancer

A few retrospective (case-control) studies reported in the mid-1990s suggested that induced abortion (the deliberate ending of a pregnancy) was associated with an increased risk of breast cancer. However, these studies had important design limitations that could have affected the results. A key limitation was their reliance on self-reporting of medical history information by the study participants, which can introduce bias. Prospective studies, which are more rigorous in design and unaffected by such bias, have consistently shown no association between induced abortion and breast cancer risk. Moreover, in 2009, the Committee on Gynecologic Practice of the American College of Obstetricians and Gynecologists concluded that "more rigorous recent studies demonstrate no causal relationship between induced abortion and a subsequent increase in breast cancer risk." Major findings from these recent studies include the following:

- Women who have had an induced abortion have the same risk of breast cancer as other women.

- Women who have had a spontaneous abortion (miscarriage) have the same risk of breast cancer as other women.

- Cancers other than breast cancer also appear to be unrelated to a history of induced or spontaneous abortion.

National Cancer Institute,
"Reproductive History and Breast Cancer Risk,"
May 10, 2011.

tion. By contrast, a person not undergoing breast cancer treatment has little reason to tell a stranger she once decided to terminate a pregnancy.

In 1994, a paper in the *Journal of the National Cancer Institute* drew the public's attention—and fire. After interviewing 845 women who had a breast cancer diagnosis at age 45 or younger, as well as 961 "control" subjects, researchers led by Janet Daling of Seattle's Fred Hutchinson Cancer Center observed a 50 percent higher risk of breast cancer among women who admitted to having had an abortion. (The association didn't hold for women who said they'd had a miscarriage.) Anti-abortion groups like the National Right to Life trumpeted the report. In an accompanying editorial, epidemiologist Lynn Rosenberg acknowledged the relevance of "reproductive factors" in breast cancer development, but faulted the study's reliance on personal, emotionally charged interviews.

A Political Debate

The debate moved from women's health to the political realm. Some on the left, such as Michael Castleman in *Mother Jones*, posited that pro-abortion rights interests risked credibility by ignoring data. The *Economist* countered this line of thinking with an article on "Abortion, breast cancer and the misuse of epidemiology." Fear played in all too readily. Sociologist Barry Glassner recalls bus banner ads in Baltimore proclaiming, "Women who choose abortion suffer more and deadlier breast cancer."

What might have settled the question was a 1997 *New England Journal of Medicine* report. This gigantic analysis of more than 1.5 million Danish women didn't involve interviews. The investigators culled data from Denmark's Civil Registration System, Cancer Registry, and mandatory abortion records. They found no correlation, period. More than a few women, [health writer] Jane Brody in the *New York Times* among them, expressed relief and hope that the study's comprehensive scope and reliable data might "put to rest a long-standing concern."

It didn't. Controversy persisted to such a degree that in July 2002, the National Cancer Institute [NCI] responded to a nudge from congressional conservatives by changing information on its website. Pro-abortion rights lawmakers charged the agency with distorting and suppressing scientific information for ideological reasons. After some back-and-forth and a congressional investigation, the institute convened geneticists, epidemiologists, oncologists, and other experts to review all evidence. The conclusion rests on an NCI fact sheet: Elective abortions are not associated with an increased risk of breast cancer.

An Upending of Informed Consent

The ethical principle of informed consent means this: A patient should know, and understand as best possible, the likely risks and benefits of a medical procedure before signing on. Now, at least five states sponsor misleading, partisan-promoted material on abortion and breast cancer risk.

Around the country, new choice-cramping laws are in the works. Many of the proposed informational mandates exploit the concept of informed consent to assure its opposite: promulgation of untruths about abortion. These bills appeal, falsely, to reason—with smart-sounding, progressive-seeming phrases, like "a right to know." They feed on women's fear of a dreaded disease. Few pregnant women are sufficiently versed in science or statistics to refute their lawmakers' misconceptions.

The bottom line is that most breast cancer cases go unexplained. There are infinite variables in an ordinary woman's life. If I were to counsel a woman contemplating an abortion, that's what I'd say. We know too little.

| "Less than one percent of women getting a medication-induced abortion at Planned Parenthood had a serious side effect or a failed abortion, according to a new study."

Medical Abortions Are Safe

Genevra Pittmann

In the following viewpoint Genevra Pittman argues that the results of medical abortions study show that there is very little risk involved in medical abortions. Pittman points to a study involving 233,805 women that use medical abortion. Based on the small percentage of serious side effects, the author concludes that medical abortion is a good, safe abortion option and can be used as an alternative to the more common surgical ones. Pittmann is a Senior Editor at Reuters Health.

As you read, consider the following questions:

1. According to the author, how many women in the 233,805 person study had a serious side effect related to medical abortion?

2. According to the author, what percent of US counties have no abortion provider?

3. What method of abortion is the most common in the US, according to Pittmann?

Less than one percent of women getting a medication-induced abortion at Planned Parenthood had a serious side effect or a failed abortion, according to a new study.

Researchers found the rate of abortion-related complications sending women to the emergency room or requiring a blood transfusion, for example, was one in 625 during 2009 and 2010.

"At Planned Parenthood, medical abortion is extremely safe," said reproductive health researcher James Trussell from Princeton University in New Jersey, who worked on the study.

"The most common adverse outcome is just continuing pregnancy," he added. "It doesn't work 100 percent of the time."

The data came from 233,805 first-trimester abortions done using the drugs mifepristone and misoprostol at 317 Planned Parenthood health centers.

In one in 200 of those cases, women had an ongoing pregnancy that wasn't terminated after two attempts with medication, the researchers reported Thursday in Obstetrics & Gynecology.

Eight women each year had an ectopic pregnancy—when the embryo implants outside the uterus—that was diagnosed after the attempted abortion. One died from related complications.

Of the 233,805 abortions during the study period, 385 women had a serious side effect, including 238 who sought ER treatment, 135 who were admitted to the hospital, 114 who had a blood transfusion and 57 who required intravenous antibiotics. All of those women survived.

"This continues to show that medical abortion is a very, very safe option for women," said Dr. Debra Stulberg, who studies disparities in reproductive health at the University of Chicago and wasn't involved in the new study. "That's really the take-home point."

She told Reuters Health medical abortions are still less common than surgical ones in the U.S., but that they're becoming relatively more frequent and "women should be reassured" based on these and other data.

Surgical procedures are also known to be safe, researchers noted. One study from 2010 found that about one percent of women having a surgical abortion before their 16th week of pregnancy had a complication that could require intravenous fluid, and just one in 300 had a major complication.

One limitation, the study team noted, is that not all women checked back after the abortion or had follow up medical records available—so it's possible more complications could have occurred that weren't recorded.

Planned Parenthood staff members were required to make three attempts to reach any patients who didn't return for follow up visits under the organization's medical standards and guidelines.

"We assume that if anything had happened, that people would get back in touch with Planned Parenthood," Trussell told Reuters Health.

"The reason that people often skip their follow up is, they're fine."

Two of the study's authors are Planned Parenthood employees, and Trussell is a member of the National Medical Committee of Planned Parenthood Federation of America. Another author receives compensation from the U.S. distributor of mifepristone, Danco Laboratories.

The medication regimen used by Planned Parenthood—and many other abortion providers—is slightly different than

Medication Abortion

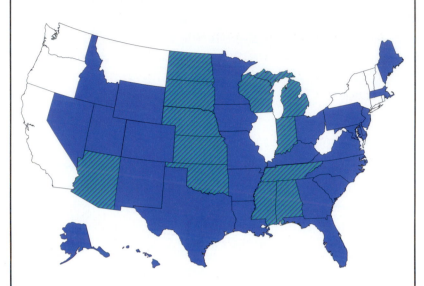

■ Mifepristone must be provided by a licensed physician

▨ Mifepristone must be provided by a licensed physician in the physical presence of the patient

Caveats and additional requirements:

Alabama: Law requiring physical presence of patient is scheduled to go into effect later in 2013.

Arizona: Requires mifepristone be provided using the FDA medication protocol. Regulations to be developed.

Indiana: Law requiring physical presence of patient is scheduled to go into effect later in 2013.

Mississippi: Law requiring physical presence of patient is scheduled to go into effect later in 2013.

North Dakota: Also requires mifepristone be provided using the FDA medication protocol. Enforcement temporarily enjoined by court order; policies are not in effect, pending the outcome of litigation.

Ohio: Requires mifepristone be provided using the FDA medication protocol.

Oklahoma: Law requires mifepristone be provided using the FDA medication protocol. Enforcement permanently enjoined by court order; policy not in effect.

Texas: Law allows for mifepristone to be by provided following the medication levels recommended by the American Congress of Obstetricians and Gynecologists, as of January 1, 2013.

TAKEN FROM: Guttmacher Intiture, "State Policies in Brief: Medication Abortion," December 1, 2013.

the U.S. Food and Drug Administration-approved drug course because it includes lower doses of mifepristone and at-home use of misoprostol.

There have been attempts in some states to force providers to use the approved regimen, according to Trussell, even though so-called off-label use of the drugs is allowed. There's no evidence the FDA regimen is safer, he said—but it is more expensive.

"It has nothing to do with medicine," he said. "It's just nuisance."

Medical abortions done at Planned Parenthood run for about $300 to $800, according to its website.

The researchers said their findings don't support laws restricting the drugs' use.

"Mandating the FDA-approved regimen, without a scientific basis, does not protect patients from unsafe abortion; it only limits access to safe and effective medical abortion for women desiring a pregnancy termination," they concluded.

"[The abortion-causing drug] RU-486 ... has resulted in thousands of complications including deaths."

Abortion-Causing Drugs Are Dangerous to Women

Wendy Wright

In the following viewpoint Wendy Wright argues against US Food and Drug Administration (FDA) approval of Ella, a drug intended to prevent pregnancy. Wright claims that Ella has similar dangers to mifepristone, formerly called RU-486, which is used to induce abortion. Additionally, Wright claims that Ella can induce abortion in some cases. Wright contends that the failure of other morning-after pills should act as a cautionary tale against Ella. Wright is former president and CEO of Concerned Women for America, a public policy women's organization that aims to bring biblical principles into all levels of public policy.

As you read, consider the following questions:

1. According to Wright, in what way is the drug Ella similar to mifepristone, or RU-486?

2. In what way does Wright claim that users of Ella could be misled and denied full information?

3. The author claims that prior to approval of the morning-after pill Plan B, abortion proponents claimed that abortion could be reduced by what percentage?

Should a drug that is similar to RU-486, the abortion drug, be approved as a morning-after pill? The Food and Drug Administration (FDA) will decide whether to approve ulipristal acetate (under the brand name Ella) as a prescription drug to be used up to five days after intercourse.

Ulipristal, or Ella, is similar to mifepristone (RU-486), a drug that causes an abortion. If the FDA approves Ella [which was approved in August 2010], it will combine the serious medical and ethical issues of RU-486 with the troubling problems of the morning-after pill.

FDA Hearings on the Drug

At an FDA Advisory Committee hearing, the drug sponsor avoided answering whether the drug causes an abortion—even when repeatedly asked.

Dr. Jeffrey Bray, a pharmacologist at the Food and Drug Administration, said that Ella may both delay ovulation and prohibit embryos from implantation in the uterus. Dr. Scott Emerson, a member of the FDA Advisory Committee and professor of biostatistics at the University of Washington, pressed the drug sponsor on why Ella is more effective the later it is taken. He asserted that any drug must do more than delay ovulation if it can prevent pregnancy up to five days after sex.

Despite this, the panel voted unanimously not to inform people that the drug can do something other than prevent pregnancy by delaying ovulation and that it may cause an abortion. Dr. Melissa Gilliam stated there should be "no extra burdens due to the mechanism of action."

While the drug sponsor, HRA Pharma, is not currently requesting non-prescription access, approval of the drug is the first step to gaining such status. Advocates of "reproductive health" have forthrightly stated that their goal is to make abortion easily and directly accessible without medical oversight or safety protocols.

Dr. Valerie Montgomery Rice, an FDA panel member and dean of Meharry Medical College, insisted the drug should be over-the-counter [OTC], asking, "Why would we not move to O.T.C. status?"

The Dangers of Medication Abortion

Ella operates in the same manner as the abortion drug RU-486 by blocking progesterone receptors. RU-486 was approved without adequate trials and, even with restricted distribution, has resulted in thousands of complications including deaths. Over one thousand adverse events from RU-486 have been reported to the FDA. The most frequent were hemorrhage and infection. Most disturbing are seven deaths. In addition, as of 2006, the FDA reported nine life-threatening incidents, 232 hospitalizations, 116 blood transfusions, and 88 cases of infection. This is the minimum number since many people, including doctors, are not willing or unaware of how to report adverse events.

A series of deaths linked to RU-486 of previously healthy women from a rare form of bacterial infection forced the FDA to convene a medical symposium to investigate. The FDA did not foresee this fatal complication, perhaps because the appropriate trials and information were not required or submitted to the FDA prior to its approval of RU-486.

Even though the FDA placed restrictions on administering RU-486, abortion providers flagrantly violated the protocol. Planned Parenthood openly posts its deviations from the FDA's protocol on its websites. (Holly Patterson, a healthy 18-year-old, died from a Planned Parenthood administered RU-486 abortion. She had visited the organization's website, where it claimed that RU-486 was "extremely safe.") FDA officials could not or would not enforce their restrictions.

The lesson is quite clear: abortion providers, or those who seek to cause an abortion on a woman, are willing to ignore FDA guidelines and endanger women's lives and health. Instituting regulations on a drug that can end a pregnancy will not restrain those who are intent on aborting a woman's baby. While advocates for RU-486 may claim it is safe, the families of the women who died from the drug will beg to differ.

The Dangers of the Morning-After Pill

The clinical trials looked at by the European Medicines Agency (EMA) reported on a single dose per menstrual cycle in a limited group of women. In the real world, it will be used more frequently and by all types of females. Of particular concern are adolescents and those less capable of understanding the complicated language on a drug label (i.e. non-English speakers). Women or girls who are fearful of a pregnancy will be inclined to take a double dose or repeated doses within a month, going to different doctors or pharmacies if necessary.

EMA noticed an effect on all tissues, particularly the liver, "if the drug is used again a month later. Most likely this has no implications, because ulipristal acetate is given as a single dose, but in repeated dose this could result in toxicity due to accumulation."

The clinical trials report a pattern of infections and bleeding disturbances that are similar to the complications reported for RU-486. Pain and bleeding are also the warning signals of an ectopic pregnancy. One known RU-486 fatality was a patient who died from a ruptured ectopic pregnancy. Brenda Vise called the abortion provider numerous times to report pain and bleeding. She was told these are the usual effects of RU-486 and not to go to a hospital. By the time she went to a hospital, it was too late. Women taking Ella may mistake the signs of an ectopic pregnancy and not receive critical medical care.

The subjects in the clinical trials were females 16 years and older. However, if Ella is approved, it will be taken by girls younger than 16. Adolescents are especially vulnerable to relying on it as a regular form of birth control, because they generally don't plan ahead or don't want to admit they're regularly having sex.

Also missing in the trials are women with anemia or respiratory disease and women who are already using hormonal contraceptives who may take Ella for missed pills. The selected subjects do not reflect the widespread types of women who will use the drug who think that an FDA approval assures it is safe for all women.

The Drug's Effect on a Pregnancy

The lack of adequate trials leaves open the question as to whether Ella is teratogenic and what kinds of birth defects it may cause in surviving or subsequent pregnancies. In the Phase III trials, 49 of the women who took Ella became pregnant, 31 had induced abortions, 11 had spontaneous abortions, two had live births (one baby suffered optic nerve hypoplasia and developmental delay), and five were lost to follow-up. There was no indication if the babies who were aborted or miscarried suffered defects.

The EMA admitted, "Extremely limited data are available on the health of the foetus/new-born in case a pregnancy is exposed to ulipristal acetate." It also noted, "The safety for a human embryo is unknown."

Although voting unanimously on the drug's safety, several panel members expressed concern that there is not enough information on the drug's effect on a pregnancy.

But then the FDA panel "strongly recommended" that the FDA not require a pregnancy test before taking the drug, instead making women rely on a doctor's opinion on whether they're pregnant.

Why would the panel insist on not ensuring that a woman is not pregnant before taking Ella? It's possible a woman could be pregnant from a previous sexual encounter. Why do they want women and researchers to be in the dark, not fully certain whether she is pregnant when she takes Ella? Perhaps to avert liability from the drug company if a woman later miscarries, her surviving baby suffers health issues or to deceive women on whether Ella caused them to abort a baby.

If Ella is approved, there is no adequate reporting mechanism to ascertain the numbers and kinds of complications women or their surviving and subsequent babies are likely to experience. This can leave the false impression that the drug is safe and effective when, in reality, complications are not reported or made available for women to make an informed decision.

One FDA committee member, Dr. Melissa Gilliam, argued against long-term studies on pregnancy outcomes. She claimed it would be "biased" because people who experience a negative effect are more likely to report. This reveals a deep distrust of women and allowing women to have full information. While researchers may want statistical minutiae, mothers care more about what kind of effect a drug may have on their baby.

The FDA panel exposes the radical view of many in the "reproductive health" community who view pregnancy as the worst possible condition, and any negative effect caused by a drug on women and babies is merely collateral damage.

Interestingly, the panel chairman, Dr. Sandra Carson, strongly recommended that the drug label restrict use by lactating mothers. This clearly indicates that she believes the drug could have an effect on a nursing baby. It's only common sense, then, that babies *in utero*, receiving nutrition and oxygen from their mothers, may also be affected by the drug.

Ella's Abortifacient Effect

Ella blocks progesterone receptors, causing a hostile environment for an embryo by interfering with the uterine lining so that an embryo cannot implant or, if implanted, not receive nutrition.

The EMA states, "Ella is contra-indicated during an existing or suspected pregnancy." However, most women would not know if they are pregnant at an early phase of the pregnancy.

If Ella is easy to obtain, it will be used past 120 hours. A large selling point of Ella is the claim that it is effective for a longer time postcoitally [after intercourse] than [the drug known as] Plan B. Women and predators will be enticed to use it beyond 120 hours, putting the woman at greater risk of aborting an implanted embryo (by any definition, a pregnancy).

Women who are led to believe that Ella is a "morning-after pill" may find out too late it may have aborted their baby, causing them emotional and psychological harm. Not providing women full information will be viewed as a deliberate effort to manipulate women for profit or ideological purposes.

The Abuse of Reproductive Drugs

If Ella is easy to obtain, woman will be victims to it being slipped to them without their consent. A pattern of abuse has already emerged with abortion-inducing drugs.

Reports (compiled by Life Issues Institute, LifeNews, LifeSiteNews and Concerned Women for America) include:

- In 2007, a 21-year-old Virginia man was sentenced to five years in prison for trying to poison his girlfriend with the intent of trying to cause an abortion. Daniel Riase crushed two misoprostol pills and put them into 19-year-old Sharii Best's drink, after which she began to bleed. She went to the hospital, where her 11-week pregnancy ended in miscarriage. She later discovered an e-mail receipt for his purchase of the drug.

- In 2007, a 34-year-old Wisconsin man named Manish Patel was arrested and charged with attempted first-degree homicide of an unborn child for trying to cause the abortion of his unborn twins. He obtained mifepristone (RU-486) from his native India and put it in his girlfriend's drink. Darshana Patel never drank the spiked drink, but turned it over to the authorities after suspecting foul play. Testing confirmed the presence of the drug. She believes a previous miscarriage was also caused by Manish slipping the drug in her drink.

- In 2009 in Alaska, Airman First Class Scott Boie faced a court martial for causing his wife to have an abortion. He did a computer search and got a friend to obtain misoprostol for him. He crushed up the pills and put them in his wife Caylinn's food. She miscarried a week later, thinking it occurred naturally. She learned about his actions from a friend.

- In 2010, 38-year-old New York pharmacist Orbin Eeli Tercero was arrested for causing his Pennsylvania girlfriend to have an abortion. He allegedly inserted misoprostol tablets vaginally during two sexual encounters. He also dissolved misoprostol tablets in her drinks. As she started miscarrying, she discovered the partially dissolved pill in her discharge. He is charged with the murder of an unborn child in the first degree.

- In 2010, 31-year-old Jered Ahlstrom from Utah pleaded guilty to unlawful termination of his girlfriend's pregnancy. He put misoprostol in her food twice to cause an abortion. She delivered a 16-week stillborn baby. He later admitted over e-mail that he had caused her abortion.

• In 2007, a 25-year-old Maryland man, William Stanley Sutton, spiked his girlfriend's drink in an attempt to cause an abortion. He used a cattle hormone sometimes used to cause abortions in cows. Lauren Ashley Tucker went to the hospital complaining of a possible poisoning after consuming the foul drink that burned her throat. Both she and her 15-week-old unborn baby survived. He was charged with reckless endangerment, assault, and contaminating her drink.

• The girlfriend of a Canadian man, Gary Bourgeois, refused to have an abortion. During sexual relations, he inserted misoprostol. Later she experienced violent cramps, then felt a partly dissolved pill drop from her vagina. Her baby died. In September 2003, he pleaded guilty to aggravated assault and administering a noxious substance.

• Dr. Stephen Pack pled guilty to injecting Joy Schepis with an abortion-inducing drug in April 2000. The New York doctor jabbed his former lover with a syringe filled with [an abortion-causing drug] methotrexate to cause an abortion because she refused to have one.

These cases are known because charges were filed. No one knows how many other women suffered "miscarriages" or abortions forced upon them by someone else.

The EMA assumed a warning on a label that "use of ulipristal acetate is not recommended in females with severe hepatic impairment, is . . . considered sufficient." The EMA also restricts use by those with severe asthma. Label warnings of contra-indications will not necessarily deter a predator whose goal is to prevent or end a woman's pregnancy.

Easy to access abortion drugs, while touted as giving women more control over their bodies, are just as easily used by men to exploit women.

The Potential Abuse of Minors

Minors who are sexually active are oftentimes victims of sexual abuse. Interaction with medical professionals is an important line of defense. Making Ella easy to obtain will remove a critical opportunity for abused minors to get the real help that they need.

The Alan Guttmacher Institute reported: "The younger women are when they first have intercourse the more likely they are to have had unwanted or nonvoluntary first sex, seven in 10 of those who had sex before age 13, for example."

"The possibility of sexual abuse should be considered routinely in every adolescent female patient who has initiated sexual activity," stated [former US surgeon general] Dr. Jocelyn Elders in the *Journal of the American Medical Association*. The rush to choose "pregnancy outcome options" may preempt efforts to rule out sexual abuse. "Sexual abuse is a common antecedent of adolescent pregnancy, with up to 66% of pregnant teens reporting histories of abuse. . . . Pregnancy may also be a sign of ongoing sexual abuse. . . . [researchers] found that of 535 young women who were pregnant, 44% had been raped, of whom 11% became pregnant as a result of the rape. One half of these young women with rape histories were raped more than once."

Approval of Morning-After Pill

Many lessons can be learned from the approval of the morning-after pill Plan B—and should not be repeated.

Advocates for the morning-after pill claimed that it would dramatically reduce pregnancies and abortions. Planned Parenthood states that the morning-after pill "could prevent 1.7 million unintended pregnancies and 800,000 abortions each year in the U.S." That would mean reducing abortions by fifty percent. Claims like this won support inside and outside the FDA, yet the reality is quite different.

Advocates have since admitted that easy access to the morning-after pill does not reduce pregnancies or abortions.

Dr. James Trussell, an aggressive proponent of "emergency contraceptive pills" (ECP), concluded in several studies subsequent to the FDA's approval that easy access to the morning-after pill has not reduced pregnancies or abortions. His most recent analysis in May 2010 stated, "No published study has yet demonstrated that increasing access to ECPs can reduce pregnancy or abortion rates in a population although one demonstration project and three clinical trials were specifically designed to address this issue." This is true even when women are given advance supplies of the drug.

Concerned Women for America had warned that easy access to the morning-after pill would not reduce pregnancies or abortions, but lead to women relying on it (the least effective form of contraception) as a regular form of birth control and multiple use.

Dr. Trussell reluctantly admits that "reanalysis of one of the randomized trials suggests that easier access to ECPs may have increased the frequency of coital acts with the potential to lead to pregnancy. Women in the increased access group were significantly more likely to report that they had ever used emergency contraception because they did not want to use either condoms or another contraceptive method. Increased access to ECPs had a greater impact on repeat use among women who were at lower baseline risk of pregnancy."

Moreover, previous studies (certainly some that the FDA relied on) miscalculated estimates of the effectiveness of morning-after pills. As Dr. Trussell put it, "The risk of pregnancy for women requesting ECPs appears to be lower than assumed in the estimates of ECP efficacy, which are consequently likely to be overestimates."

Ideology Trumps Women's Health

Abortion advocates cloak abortion-causing drugs as a woman's "right." This is a facade used to promote their own ideological crusade.

With Ella, women will be enticed to buy a poorly tested abortion drug under the guise that it's a morning-after pill.

The FDA should not unleash Ella on unsuspecting women, a drug promoted by activists with a history of overstating the efficacy of reproductive drugs while understating the overall risks to women.

> *"The United States practices its own form of selective abortion when it comes to fetuses diagnosed in utero with Down syndrome and other chromosomal conditions."*

Selective Abortion Is Influenced by Discriminatory Attitudes Toward Disability

Amy Julia Becker

In the following viewpoint Amy Julia Becker argues that the decision to abort fetuses with Down syndrome and other disabling conditions is prejudiced by attitudes toward disability. Becker claims that the propensity in the United States to abort fetuses with Down syndrome is not wholly unlike the decision in many parts of the world to abort female fetuses. Becker is the author of What Every Woman Needs to Know About Prenatal Testing: Insight from a Mom Who Has Been There *and* A Good and Perfect Gift: Faith, Expectations, and a Little Girl Named Penny.

As you read, consider the following questions:

1. What factors does the author identify that contribute to the decision around the globe to abort girls?

2. Becker claims that the life expectancy of people born with Down syndrome now is what?

3. According to the author, in what region of the United States are fetuses with Down syndrome most likely to be diagnosed and terminated?

In her Pulitzer Prize–nominated book *Unnatural Selection: Choosing Boys over Girls and the Consequences of a World Full of Men*, journalist Mara Hvistendahl takes a close look at the distorted sex ratios among the populations of China and India. Hvistendahl writes, "Sex selection has resulted in an imbalance of over 100 million more men than women worldwide." Inexpensive ultrasound technology has enabled this imbalance as couples can now learn whether they are having boys or girls and respond with "selective abortions" if having a girl seems undesirable.

Social Conditions and Abortion

Social conditions and systemic bias against women contribute to the millions of couples worldwide who choose against giving birth to a girl. As the *Economist* explained a few years back, "Perhaps hard physical labour is still needed for the family to make its living. Perhaps only sons may inherit land. Perhaps a daughter is deemed to join another family on marriage and you want someone to care for you when you are old. Perhaps she needs a dowry." Social conditions, economic reality, even the prospect of being able to provide adequate long-term care—all of these factors contribute to the decision to abort girls.

In the West we decry these practices as gendercide, but the United States practices its own form of selective abortion when it comes to fetuses diagnosed in utero with Down syndrome and other chromosomal conditions. Definitive numbers related to pregnancies terminated as a result of a prenatal diagnosis of Down syndrome are hard to come by. Older studies suggest that up to 90 percent of all pregnant women with a definitive prenatal diagnosis chose abortion. As Jamie Natali, et al. demonstrated in the *Journal of Prenatal Diagnosis*, more recent studies put the number closer to 70 percent. Either way, women who learn through prenatal testing that their fetuses have Down syndrome often decide to abort, and their reasons aren't that different from the reasons women across the globe choose (or are forced) to abort girls. In India, daughters grow up with social stigma, a lack of educational opportunities and the prospect of becoming a burden to their parents. Substitute the words "America" and "children with Down syndrome" for "India" and "daughters," and you get the picture.

Down syndrome occurs upon conception when an embryo receives three copies of chromosome 21 instead of the typical pair. This additional chromosome can lead to physical differences such as shortened stature, an extra fold of skin around the eyes, small facial features, and pronated [flat] feet. It can also lead to medical concerns that vary from person to person but include heart defects, hearing deficits, and a heightened risk of childhood leukemia, hyperthyroidism, and celiac disease. Down syndrome also usually involves some unpredictable degree of intellectual disability, so many individuals with Down syndrome have greater challenges to overcome when learning or when trying to live independently as adults.

Bias in the Decision to Abort

It is precisely because of information like this that many people choose to abort a fetus diagnosed with Down syndrome. These medical and social challenges seem fixed and unchanging. But as the past 40 years demonstrates, these challenges reflect social mores and choices as much as biologically-based reality or necessity. In 1975, Congress ensured all children's rights to a free public education, including those

Incidence of Down Syndrome

Maternal Age	Incidence of Down Syndrome	Maternal Age	Incidence of Down Syndrome
20	1 in 2,000	35	1 in 350
21	1 in 1,700	36	1 in 300
22	1 in 1,500	37	1 in 250
23	1 in 1,400	38	1 in 200
24	1 in 1,300	39	1 in 150
25	1 in 1,200	40	1 in 100
26	1 in 1,100	41	1 in 80
27	1 in 1,050	42	1 in 70
28	1 in 1,000	43	1 in 50
29	1 in 950	44	1 in 40
30	1 in 900	45	1 in 30
31	1 in 800	46	1 in 25
32	1 in 720	47	1 in 20
33	1 in 600	48	1 in 15
34	1 in 450	49	1 in 10

TAKEN FROM: National Down Syndrome Society, "What is Down Syndrome?" accessed June 17, 2013. www.ndss.org.

with intellectual disabilities. Around that same time, parents on the whole stopped sending their kids with Down syndrome to institutions and availed themselves of "early intervention," therapy services that target physical and brain development from very early on in a baby's life. In 1980 the life expectancy for an infant with Down syndrome was 25. As a result of social change and medical advances, people with Down syndrome are now expected to live until at least 60. And people with Down syndrome overcome expectations every day. They read, they write, they go to work, they make friends. When given the opportunity, they lead lives of hope and promise.

Although most women with a prenatal diagnosis of Down syndrome choose to terminate, even within the United States demographic differences demonstrate the socially-construed nature of these personal choices. A broad study by James Egan, et al. in the *Journal of Prenatal Testing* analyzed demographic differences in Down syndrome livebirths in the United States from 1989 to 2006. As the study records, "a Down syndrome fetus is more likely to be prenatally diagnosed and terminated in the West and least likely to be diagnosed and terminated in the Midwest" and, "women with 12 or fewer years of education were less likely to either receive a prenatal diagnosis of Down syndrome or terminate an affected fetus compared to women with 13 or more years of education." In other words, social context affects the decision to abort.

Americans recognize the discriminatory nature of allowing sex to determine the value of a human life. We should also recognize the discriminatory attitudes that can lead to selective abortion in our own country. There has never been a better time to be born with Down syndrome, medically, educationally, and socially. We can overcome the residual cultural bias towards individuals with intellectual and physical disabilities not through pregnancy termination but through social supports, inclusive classrooms, and a culture that recognizes the distinct contributions offered by each individual.

| *"There are times when abortion is the humane choice."*

Selective Abortion to Avoid Disability Is Sometimes the Humane Choice

Frances Ryan

In the following viewpoint Frances Ryan argues that the campaign in Great Britain to make it illegal to terminate a pregnancy solely on the grounds of disability is a misguided campaign. Ryan claims that sometimes abortion is the humane choice for both the fetus and the prospective parents. She concludes that women should continue to be allowed to make their own decisions about abortion and disability, and she suggests a better way to help make society better for the disabled and their families. Ryan is a columnist for the New Statesman *and writes regularly for the British daily newspaper* The Guardian.

As you read, consider the following questions:

1. The author claims that campaigners aiming to ban abortion in the case of disability noted the contradiction in abortion law highlighted by what event?

2. According to Ryan, what percentage of couples in England and Wales choose abortion after discovering the fetus has Down syndrome?

3. Instead of banning abortion in the case of disability, the author suggests what social changes?

Disability and abortion are two words not without a creeping discomfort. More so, when put together. The latter recently reared its head; casual calls to draw back a woman's right to choose are now familiar in their cyclicality. The Tory [Britain's Conservative Party] minister for women Maria Miller, for her part, would like to reduce the abortion time limit to 20 weeks. Despite the fact that this is the point when many foetal abnormalities are detected, Miller, the former minister for disabled people, made no mention of what it would mean for women whose 20-week scan showed their child would have a disability. She either hadn't thought it through or didn't much care.

The Campaign to Ban Certain Abortions

Some people seem to care, often more than they should. Last month [September 2012], an alliance of "pro-life" campaigners and religious groups launched a campaign to ban the termination of pregnancies on the grounds of disability. The Paralympics—with its "astonishing examples of courage and triumphs over disability"—they said, highlighted the "contradiction" in the current abortion law.

The contradiction they refer to is that while the Abortion Act 1967 sets a 24-week limit on having an abortion, when there is "substantial risk that if the child were born, she or he would have physical or mental abnormalities as to be seriously handicapped", there is no limit. There are good reasons for that—medicine, practicality and basic human empathy.

Last year [2011], out of the almost 190,000 abortions in England and Wales, 146 of them were after the 24-week point.

However, the percentage of couples who choose an abortion after discovering their baby will have Down's syndrome is routinely 90%. For some, being told their child will have a severe disability is reason enough not to go ahead with the pregnancy. Worse (if certain moral judgments are to be applied), this is sometimes the case for pregnancies resulting from IVF [in vitro fertilization] that, before the word "disabled" was uttered, were much wanted.

A Humane Choice

Those trying to ban abortions on disability grounds claim that this is "eugenics," a form of "disability discrimination." And they think a sporting event that displays the most physically able disabled people tells us all we need to know about disability and, while we're at it, a woman's decision-making process. These are campaigners who reduce the nuances of disability to an insulting level, yet speak as if they are saving us from being wiped out, and we should be grateful.

There are times when abortion is the humane choice. In reality, there are times when people feel they simply cannot cope. It's OK to say that out loud. The thought doesn't suggest a disabled life is worth less, but acknowledges the extra time, energy and money a severely disabled life needs. Right now, there are parents of disabled children who are having to skip meals to pay the gas bill. There are disabled children who aren't getting the childcare, schools, therapies or even healthcare they need. If aborting a disabled foetus makes you uncomfortable, perhaps that should too.

It's convenient to judge the individual choosing the abortion. Truth is, many make their choice based on the conditions of society. To care about disability means working to make these changes, not using it as a smokescreen to take women's rights.

Periodical and Internet Source Bibliography

The following articles have been selected to supplement the diverse views presented in this chapter.

Bob Beauprez	"Reconciling *Roe v. Wade*," Townhall, January 22, 2013. www.townhall.com.
Steve Hall	"A Birth Defect Shouldn't Be a Death Sentence," *World*, January 25, 2013.
Connie Mackey	"Women Are Not Better Off Because of Abortion," *US News and World Report*, January 22, 2013.
Jeanne Monahan	"RU-486: Ten Years After," *Human Events*, September 28, 2010.
NARAL Pro-Choice America	"The Safety of Legal Abortion and the Hazards of Illegal Abortion," January 1, 2011. www.prochoiceamerica.org.
George Neumayr	"The State of the Culture of Death: The Gosnell Case and What *Roe* Has Wrought," *Catholic World Report*, March 2011.
Michael New	"Abortion Laws and Their Effects on Abortion Rates," Family Research Council One Pager, July 2010. www.frc.org.
Kyle-Anne Shiver	"The Coverup of Abortion's Real Risks," *American Thinker*, April 11, 2011. www.americanthinker.com.
Cal Thomas	"*Roe v. Wade* at 40," *World*, January 22, 2013.
Robert VerBruggen	"The Truth About Abortion," *National Review Online*, January 21, 2011. www.nationalreview.com.

For Further Discussion

Chapter 1

1. Mary Elizabeth Williams claims that the life of the woman always trumps the life of the fetus, so that she may choose abortion. How might Doug Bandow argue that even if it is true that the life of the woman trumps the life of the fetus, this would only justify abortion in limited circumstances?

2. Both Ann Furedi and Karen Swallow Prior emphasize the importance of the moral agency, or moral will, of women. Yet, they come to conflicting conclusions regarding how this justifies the choice to abort a pregnancy. What is the core of their disagreement regarding the importance of moral agency?

Chapter 2

1. William Sullivan argues that *Roe v. Wade* should be overturned, saying that abortion is "acceptible for the same reasons slavery was tolerated: both the slave and the unborn are not considered full 'persons.'" Does Michael C. Dorf succeed in refuting Sullivan's arguments against *Roe*? Why or why not?

2. Eleanor J. Bader, Steve Erickson, and Daniel Allott all discuss the political climate after *Roe v. Wade*. Drawing on one or more of these viewpoints, do you think the decision caused more benefits or more harms? Explain your answer.

Chapter 3

1. Both Douglas Johnson and Christy Zink discuss the issue of pain as morally relevant. What specific difference in their thinking causes them to take opposing viewpoints on the issue of abortion after twenty weeks?

2. After considering the viewpoints of Mary E. Harned and Nina Liss-Shultz, do you think minors should be allowed to obtain abortions without parental involvement? Support your answer by drawing on either of the viewpoints.

Chapter 4

1. Amy Julia Becker worries about how discrimination affects attitudes toward abortion, and Frances Ryan contends that abortion is sometimes the humane choice in the case of disability. Despite certain differences in their viewpoints, on what point do they both wholeheartedly agree?

Organizations to Contact

The editors have compiled the following list of organizations concerned with the issues debated in this book. The descriptions are derived from materials provided by the organizations. All have publications or information available for interested readers. The list was compiled on the date of publication of the present volume; names, addresses, phone and fax numbers, and e-mail and Internet addresses may change. Be aware that many organizations take several weeks or longer to respond to inquiries, so allow as much time as possible.

Advocates for Youth

2000 M St. NW, Ste. 750, Washington, DC   20036
(202) 419-3420 • fax: (202) 419-1448
website: www.advocatesforyouth.org

Advocates for Youth is an organization that works both in the United States and in developing countries with a sole focus on adolescent reproductive and sexual health. Advocates for Youth champions efforts that help young people make informed and responsible decisions about their reproductive and sexual health through its core values of rights, respect, and responsibility. Advocates for Youth publishes numerous informational essays available on its website, including "Adolescents and Abortion."

American Center for Law and Justice (ACLJ)

PO Box 90555, Washington, DC   20090-0555
(800) 296-4529
website: www.aclj.org

The American Center for Law and Justice is dedicated to the idea that religious freedom and freedom of speech are inalienable, God-given rights. The ACLJ has participated in numerous cases before the US Supreme Court, federal court of appeals, federal district courts, and various state courts regarding freedom of religion and freedom of speech. The ACLJ has numerous memos and position papers available on its website, including the memo "Federal Healthcare Funding and Abortion."

American Civil Liberties Union (ACLU)
125 Broad St., 18th Fl., New York, NY   10004
(212) 549-2500
e-mail: infoaclu@aclu.org
website: www.aclu.org

The American Civil Liberties Union is a national organization that works to defend Americans' civil rights as guaranteed in the US Constitution. The ACLU works in courts, legislatures, and communities to defend First Amendment rights, the right to equal protection, the right to due process, and the right to privacy. The ACLU publishes the semiannual newsletter *Civil Liberties Alert*, as well as briefing papers, including, "The Right to Choose: A Fundamental Liberty."

American Life League (ALL)
PO Box 1350, Stafford, VA   22555
(540) 659-4171 • fax: (540) 659-2586
website: www.all.org

The American Life League is a Catholic organization that opposes abortion. ALL sponsors a number of outreach efforts designed to focus attention on individual pro-life concerns. ALL provides brochures, videos, and newsletters at its website, including the brochure "A Person's a Person, No Matter How Small."

Catholics for Choice (CFC)
1436 U St. NW, Ste. 301, Washington, DC   20009-3997
(202) 986-6093 • fax: (202) 332-7995
e-mail: cfc@catholicsforchoice.org
website: www.catholicsforchoice.org

Catholics for Choice is a Catholic organization that supports a woman's moral and legal right to follow her conscience in matters of sexuality and reproductive health. The CFC works in the United States and internationally to ensure that all people have access to safe and affordable reproductive health care. The CFC publishes *Conscience* magazine and various articles, including "In Good Conscience: Respecting the Beliefs of Health-Care Providers and the Needs of Patients."

Center for Reproductive Rights
120 Wall St., New York, NY   10005
(917) 637-3600 • fax: (917) 637-3666
e-mail: info@reprorights.org
website: www.reproductiverights.org

The Center for Reproductive Rights is a global legal advocacy organization dedicated to reproductive rights. The center uses the law to advance reproductive freedom as a fundamental human right that all governments are legally obligated to protect, respect, and fulfill. The Center for Reproductive Rights publishes articles, reports, and briefing papers, among which is the article "Parental Involvement Laws."

Concerned Women for America (CWA)
1015 Fifteenth St. NW, Ste. 1100, Washington, DC   20005
(202) 488-7000 • fax: (202) 488-0806
website: www.cwfa.org

Concerned Women for America is a public policy women's organization that has the goal of bringing biblical principles into all levels of public policy. The CWA focuses promoting biblical values on six core issues—family, sanctity of human life, education, pornography, religious liberty, and national sovereignty—through prayer, education, and social influence. Among the organization's brochures, fact sheets, and articles available on its website is "It's Time to Reject *Roe v. Wade* as Invincible Precedent."

Feminists for Life of America
PO Box 320667, Alexandria, VA   22320
e-mail: info@feministsforlife.org
website: www.feministsforlife.org

Feminists for Life of America is a nonsectarian, nonpartisan organization that seeks to eliminate the root causes that drive women to abortion. Feminists for Life of America provides practical resources and support shaped by feminist principles to help women avoid abortion. Feminists for Life of America publishes the *American Feminist* and articles such as "Women Deserve Better than Abortion."

Guttmacher Institute

125 Maiden Ln., 7th Fl., New York, NY   10038
(800) 355-0244 • fax: (212) 248-1951
website: www.guttmacher.org

The Guttmacher Institute works to advance sexual and reproductive health worldwide through an interrelated program of social science research, public education, and policy analysis. The institute collects and analyzes scientific evidence to make a difference in policies, programs, and medical practice. The Guttmacher Institute publishes *Guttmacher Policy Review*, available on its website, and other publications, including the monthly *State Policies in Brief*, which provides information on legislative and judicial actions affecting reproductive health, such as "An Overview of Minors' Consent Laws."

Human Life Foundation, Inc.

353 Lexington Ave., Ste. 802, New York, NY   10016
website: www.humanlifereview.com

The Human Life Foundation, Inc., is a nonprofit corporation with the goal of promoting alternatives to abortion. The Human Life Foundation works to achieve this goal through educational and charitable means. The foundation publishes the *Human Life Review*, a quarterly journal that focuses on abortion and other life issues.

Human Life International (HLI)

4 Family Life Ln., Front Royal, VA   22630
(800) 549-5433 • fax: (540) 622-6247

e-mail: hli@hli.org
website: www.hli.org

Human Life International is an international pro-life organization. With affiliates and associates in over a hundred countries, HLI trains, organizes, and equips pro-life leaders around the world. HLI publishes the monthly newsletters *Mission Report* and *FrontLines*, as well as *Pro-Life Talking Points*, among which is "Exceptions: Is Abortion Ever Permissible?"

NARAL Pro-Choice America

1156 Fifteenth St. NW, Ste. 700, Washington, DC   20005
(202) 973-3000 • fax: (202) 973-3096
website: www.naral.org

NARAL Pro-Choice America advocates for privacy and a woman's right to choose. It works to elect pro-choice candidates, lobbies Congress to protect reproductive rights, and monitors state and federal activity in the courts related to reproductive rights. NARAL Pro-Choice America publishes numerous fact sheets, including "The Difference Between Emergency Contraception and Early Abortion Options."

National Right to Life Committee (NRLC)

512 Tenth St. NW, Washington, DC   20004
(202) 626-8800
e-mail: nrlc@nrlc.org
website: www.nrlc.org

The National Right to Life Committee was established after the decision in *Roe v. Wade* (1973), with the goal of repealing the ruling. The NRLC works toward legislative reform at the national level to restrict abortion. NRLC publishes a monthly newspaper, the *National Right to Life News*, and several fact sheets, including "Teens and Abortion: Why Parents Should Know."

Planned Parenthood Federation of America
434 W. Thirty-Third St., New York, NY   10001
(212) 541-7800 • fax: (212) 245-1845
website: www.plannedparenthood.org

Planned Parenthood Federation of America is a sexual and reproductive health-care provider and advocate. Planned Parenthood works to improve women's health and safety, prevent unintended pregnancies, and advance the right and ability of individuals and families to make informed and responsible choices. On its website, Planned Parenthood offers information about birth control, as well as position papers, such as "Affordable Birth Control and Other Preventative Care."

Religious Coalition for Reproductive Choice
1413 K St. NW, 14th Fl., Washington, DC   20005
(202) 628-7700 • fax: (202) 628-7716
e-mail: info@rcrc.org
website: www.rcrc.org

The Religious Coalition for Reproductive Choice comprises national organizations from major faiths and traditions and religiously affiliated and independent religious organizations that support reproductive choice and religious freedom. The coalition uses education and advocacy to give voice to the reproductive issues of people of color, those living in poverty, and other underserved populations. The Religious Coalition for Reproductive Choice publishes a newsletter, *Faith & Choices*, and various articles such as "Believe It: Religious Americans Are Pro-choice."

Bibliography of Books

Scott Ainsworth and Thad E. Hall — *Abortion Politics in Congress: Strategic Incrementalism and Policy Change.* New York: Cambridge University Press, 2011.

Sarah Erdreich — *Generation* Roe: *Inside the Future of the Pro-choice Movement.* New York: Seven Stories, 2013.

Clarke D. Forsythe — *Abuse of Discretion: The Inside Story of* Roe v. Wade. New York: Encounter Books, 2012.

Linda Greenhouse and Reva Siegel, eds. — *Before* Roe v. Wade: *Voices That Shaped the Abortion Debate Before the Supreme Court's Ruling.* New York: Kaplan, 2010.

Johannah Haney — *The Abortion Debate: Understanding the Issues.* Berkeley Heights, NJ: Enslow, 2009.

Melissa Haussman — *Reproductive Rights and the State: Getting the Birth Control, RU-486, Morning-After Pills, and the Gardasil Vaccine to the US Market.* Santa Barbara, CA: Praeger, 2013.

David L. Hudson — *The Right to Privacy.* New York: Chelsea House, 2010.

N.E.H. Hull and Peter Charles Hoffer — Roe v. Wade: *The Abortion Rights Controversy in American History.* Lawrence: University Press of Kansas, 2010.

Carole Joffe — *Dispatches from the Abortion Wars: The Costs of Fanaticism to Doctors, Patients, and the Rest of Us*. Boston: Beacon, 2009.

Fran Moreland Johns — *Perilous Times: An Inside Look at Abortion Before—and After—Roe v. Wade*. New York: YBK, 2013.

Christopher Kaczor — *The Ethics of Abortion: Women's Rights, Human Life, and the Question of Justice*. New York: Routledge, 2011.

Anja J. Karnein — *A Theory of Unborn Life: From Abortion to Genetic Manipulation*. New York: Oxford University Press, 2012.

Patrick Lee — *Abortion & Unborn Human Life*. Washington, DC: Catholic University of America Press, 2010.

Paul Benjamin Linton — *Abortion Under State Constitutions: A State-by-State Analysis*. Durham, NC: Carolina Academic Press, 2012.

Catriona Macleod — *Adolescence, Pregnancy, and Abortion: Constructing a Threat of Degeneration*. New York: Routledge, 2010.

Monica Migliorino Miller — *Abandoned: The Untold Story of the Abortion War*. Charlotte, NC: Saint Benedict Press, 2012.

Janet Morana — *Recall Abortion: Ending the Abortion Industry's Exploitation of Women*. Charlotte, NC: Saint Benedict Press, 2013.

Michael J. Perry	*Constitutional Rights, Moral Controversy, and the Supreme Court.* New York: Cambridge University Press, 2009.
Stephen D. Schwarz, with Kiki Latimer	*Understanding Abortion: From Mixed Feelings to Rational Thought.* Lanham, MD: Lexington Books, 2012.
Stephen Singular	*The Wichita Divide: The Murder of Dr. George Tiller and the Battle over Abortion.* New York: St. Martin's, 2011.
James D. Slack	*Abortion, Execution, and the Consequences of Taking Life.* New Brunswick, NJ: Transaction, 2011.
Rickie Solinger	*Reproductive Politics: What Everyone Needs to Know.* New York: Oxford University Press, 2013.
Bonnie Steinbock	*Life Before Birth: The Moral and Legal Status of Embryos and Fetuses.* New York: Oxford University Press, 2011.
Michael Tooley, Celia Wolf-Devine, Philip E. Devine and Alison M. Jaggar	*Abortion: Three Perspectives.* New York: Oxford University Press, 2009.
Irene Vilar	*Impossible Motherhood: Testimony of an Abortion Addict.* New York: Other Press, 2009.

| Sarah Weddington | *A Question of Choice.* New York: Feminist Press, 2013. |
| Joshua C. Wilson | *The Street Politics of Abortion: Speech, Violence, and America's Culture Wars.* Stanford, CA: Stanford University Press, 2013. |

Index

A